DISCARD

Toni Morrison's Fiction

UNDERSTANDING CONTEMPORARY AMERICAN LITERATURE
Matthew J. Bruccoli, General Editor

Volumes on

Edward Albee • John Barth • Donald Barthelme • The Beats
The Black Mountain Poets • Robert Bly • Raymond Carver
Chicano Literature • Contemporary American Drama
Contemporary American Science Fiction
James Dickey • E. L. Doctorow • John Gardner
George Garrett • John Hawkes • Joseph Heller
John Irving • Randall Jarrell • William Kennedy
Ursula K. Le Guin • Denise Levertov • Bernard Malamud
Carson McCullers • Toni Morrison • Vladimir Nabokov
Joyce Carol Oates • Tim O'Brien • Flannery O'Conner
Cynthia Ozick • Walker Percy • Katherine Anne Porter
Thomas Pynchon • Theodore Roethke • Philip Roth
Mary Lee Settle • Isaac Bashevis Singer • Gary Snyder
William Stafford • Anne Tyler • Kurt Vonnegut
Tennessee Williams

Toni Morrison's Fiction

Jan Furman

University of South Carolina Press

Published in Columbia, South Carolina, by the
University of South Carolina Press

Manufactured in the United States of America

00 99 98 97 96   5 4 3 2 1

Library of Congress Cataloging-in-Publication Data

Furman, Marva Jannett.
  Toni Morrison's fiction/ Jan Furman.
     p. cm.—(Understanding contemporary American literature)
  Includes bibliographical references and index.
  ISBN 1–57003–067–7
  1. Morrison, Toni—Criticism and interpretation. 2. Women and
literature—United States—History—20th century. 3. Afro-American
women in literature. 4. Afro-Americans in literature. I. Title.
II. Series.
  PS3563.O8749Z65 1996
  813'.54—dc20   95-4423

For Jay, Senta, and Kara

CONTENTS

Editor's Preface

The volumes of *Understanding Contemporary American Literature* have been planned as guides or companions for students as well as good nonacademic readers. The editor and publisher perceive a need for these volumes because much of the influential contemporary literature makes special demands. Uninitiated readers encounter difficulty in approaching works that depart from the traditional forms and techniques of prose and poetry. Literature relies on conventions, but the conventions keep evolving; new writers form their own conventions—which in time may become familiar. Put simply, *UCAL* provides instruction in how to read certain contemporary writers—identifying and explicating their material, themes, use of language, point of view, structures, symbolism, and responses to experience.

The word *understanding* in the series title was deliberately chosen. Many willing readers lack an adequate understanding of how contemporary literature works; that is, what the author is attempting to express and the means by which it is conveyed. Although the criticism and analysis in the series have been aimed at a level of general accessibility, these introductory volumes are meant to be applied in conjunction with the works they cover. They do not provide a substitute for the works and authors they introduce, but rather prepare the reader for more profitable literary experiences.

M. J. B.

Toni Morrison's Fiction

1

UNDERSTANDING
TONI MORRISON

Career

Becoming a fiction writer was never Toni Morrison's youthful ambition. Her first novel, *The Bluest Eye* (1970), was not published until she was thirty-nine. By then she had a solid career as an editor at Random House, and before that she had taught for several years at major universities. Despite what seems to have been a slow start, Morrison has accomplished much. Since 1970 she has written six novels, a play, and a book of literary criticism; she has contributed essays and reviews to periodicals and won international acclaim. Her novels about triumphs and failures in the African-American community are praised for their sardonic wit, lyricism, compelling metaphors, and unflinching honesty.

Although Morrison's teachers saw and encouraged her creativity, Morrison resisted, preferring, as she says, reading to composing. It was not until she was a young wife and mother needing a break from routine that she joined a local writing workshop and wrote a short story in order to have something to share with the group. Many years later, as a single mother of two small children, she returned to work on that first story in order, she admits, to fill a void in her life. Working after her children were in bed and before they were awake in the mornings, she eventually turned the story into her first novel. Remembering these circumstances of her early career, Morrison is quick to challenge the stereotype of artist as recluse, single-mindedly pursuing an artistic vision. Many artists, and particularly women artists, must do several things simultaneously. In Morrison's case that has meant being a full-time parent as well as teaching, lecturing, and keeping up with her editorial duties at Random House.

Born Chloe Anthony Wofford on 18 February 1931 in Lorain, Ohio, Morrison grew up in this Lake Erie town with her parents, George and Ramah Wofford, an older sister, and two younger brothers. Morrison left Lorain in 1974 to attend Howard University (where she changed her name to Toni), but she revisits her childhood home by locating many of her stories in Ohio and other parts of the Midwest. In 1953 she earned a B.A. in English at Howard and two years later an M.A. from Cornell University. After Cornell, Morrison went to Houston, where for two years she taught English at Texas Southern University before returning to Howard as an instructor (1957–1964). During this seven-year interim she married Harold Morrison, a Jamaican, and had two sons. The marriage ended in divorce in 1964, and Morrison moved to New York. She worked there for a year as an editor at the textbook subsidiary of Random House in Syracuse before going to its trade division in New York City, where she remained until 1983. As senior editor at Random House, Morrison nourished the careers of several writers, including Toni Cade Bambara, Gayle Jones, Angela Davis, and Henry Dumas.

Morrison's literary honors include both the National Book Critics Circle Award and the American Academy and Institute of Arts and Letters Award for *Song of Solomon* (1977). *Beloved* (1987) won a Pulitzer Prize for fiction, and Morrison's latest novel, *Jazz* (1992), is a best-seller. For her collective achievements Morrison was awarded the Nobel Prize for literature in 1993. In its statement the Swedish Academy praised her as one "who in novels characterized by visionary force and poetic import, gives life to an essential aspect of American reality."[1]

Morrison has had visiting professorships at several universities, including Yale, Princeton, the State University of New York at Albany, and Bard College. She was appointed to President Carter's National Council of the Arts and elected to the American Academy and Institute of Arts and Letters. There is little doubt that Morrison's fiction and literary criticism about the black experience in America has contributed to an expansion and redefinition of the American literary canon. She is also a member (collaborating with nine other Nobel Prize winners in various categories from peace to medicine to literature) of the Academie Universelle des Cultures. Founded by President François Mitterrand, the recently formed academie was conceived as a continuing and highly visible colloquy on global matters of intellectual freedom.

Despite these successes Morrison's work has not always been received well by critics and readers. For example, *The Bluest Eye,* her first novel, was out of print by 1974, four years after its publication. (It has since been reprinted.) And before it won the Pulitzer, *Beloved* failed to win the National Book Award in 1987 as many expected. In protest forty-nine black writers published a letter in a *New York Times* advertisement suggesting that Morrison had been treated unjustly. Although her work has garnered praise in academic quarters, that praise has been qualified by those critics who have called her prose florid and self-indulgent.

Morrison admits that she reads reviews of her books, but she says they do not determine the direction of her work, which is informed only by her experience as a woman and African American and by the ancient stories of the African-American community. Unfavorable commentary on her novels often, Morrison asserts, "evolve[s] out of [a lack of understanding] of the culture, the world, the given quality out of which I write."[2] Morrison measures success not by the estimates of her critics, but rather by how well her books evoke the rhythms and cosmology of her people. "If anything I do," she says, "in the way of writing novels (or whatever I write) isn't about the village or the community or about you, then it is not about anything."[3]

Since 1989 Morrison has been the Robert F. Goheen Professor of the Humanities at Princeton University. She divides her time between Rockland County, New York, and Princeton, New Jersey.

Overview

Toni Morrison has said that she writes the kind of books she wants to read, suggesting that she chooses subjects that interest her and not necessarily subjects that are popular with readers and publishers. Sociology, polemics, explanation, faddish themes do not concern Morrison, who is aiming to express a cultural legacy. She wants her novels to have an oral, effortless quality, evoking the tribal storytelling tradition of the African griot, who recites the legendary events of generations. Her characters, too, should have a special essence: they should be ancestral and enduring. In pursuing this personal, artistic vision Morrison creates extraordinary tales of human experience that a less-independent writer would perhaps not attempt.

This is not to suggest that the only impetus for Morrison's fiction is self-gratification. Such an assertion would ignore a vital dimension of her accomplishment: enlightening her readers about themselves. In this context Morrison's novels are not just art for art's sake, but they are political as well. In fact, "the best art is political,"[4] she says, not in the pejorative meaning of political as haranguing, but as deliberately provocative. Morrison rejects the dichotomy of art and politics, insisting that art can be "unquestionably political and irrevocably beautiful at the same time."[5] She is careful to say, "I am not interested in indulging myself in some private, closed exercise of my imagination that fulfills only the obligation of my personal dreams."[6] Instead, her novels are instruments for transmitting cultural knowledge, filling a void once occupied by storytelling. They replace "those classical, mythological, archetypal stories that we heard years ago."[7] She believes in the artist's measure of responsibility for engendering cultural coherence and cohesion by retrieving and interpreting the past—what she calls "bear[ing] witness."[8] That responsibility largely informs her literary aesthetic.

Morrison's chief strategy for achieving this goal is to integrate life and art by anchoring her fiction in the folkways that echo the rhythms of African-American communal life. Her women get together in kitchens to talk about husbands and children. They do each other's hair, and they exorcise each other's demons. Her men walk the streets of Michigan and New York, congregate in pool halls, argue in barber shops, hunt possum in rural Kentucky. Her stories encode myths about flying Africans and tales of tar babies. As Trudier Harris demonstrates in a recent study, Morrison thoroughly integrates folk patterns into her fiction. "Instead of simply including isolated items of folklore, she manages to simulate the ethos of folk communities, to saturate her novels with a folk aura intrinsic to the texturing of the whole."[9] This pervasive incorporation of folk materials explains why Morrison strums such deeply satisfying chords of familiarity for many readers. Indeed, Morrison's work is "genuinely" representative of the folk. She shuns what she labels "the separate, isolated ivory tower voice"[10] of the artist. The (black) artist, for Morrison, "is not a solitary person who has no responsibility to the community."[11]

Morrison identifies with her readers and labors to achieve intimacy with them. She invites readers to share in the creative process, to work with her in constructing meaning in her books. She is the black preacher who, as she puts it, "requires his congregation to speak, to join him in the sermon, to behave in a certain way, to stand up and to weep and to cry and to accede or to change and to modify."[12] And like black music her stories should, Morrison continues, solicit a dynamic response. By avoiding defining adverbs and by allowing the reader to interpret character and incident, Morrison encourages participatory reading. There are, for example, no explicitly detailed sexual scenes in her work. As she says, she aims "to describe sexual scenes in such a way that they are not clinical, not even explicit—so that the reader brings his own sexuality to the scene and thereby participates in it in a very personal way. And owns it."[13]

This approach, of course, reflects any good writer's understanding of the necessary subtlety of imaginative writing and the reader's work of interpreting meaning. But Morrison's studied effort to elicit the reader's participation suggests a not-so-subtle emphasis upon the special relationship she shares with her audience. As storyteller she is bound to authentically represent experience as readers know it and to encourage their confirmation of and involvement in that representation.

As satisfying as this collaboration may be for the reader, it is just as challenging because Morrison's work is not predictable. While her language, metaphors, settings, and themes evoke the familiar and timeless, her characters seldom reinforce the reader's expectations—not because they are unrealistic, but because they often depict a reality that is too distressing to consider. Morrison's characters (and her readers with them) are brought to the edge of endurance and then asked to endure more; sometimes they crack. Under these conditions Morrison shows what extraordinary and unspeakable acts ordinary people are capable of committing.

Cholly, in *The Bluest Eye*, rapes his twelve-year-old daughter because he is overcome with pity and love for her; Pauline, the girl's mother, refuses to love her and loves instead the little white girl whose family employs her. As a child Sula watches with mild curiosity as her mother burns to death. Sula's grandmother Eva Peace sets fire to her drug-addicted son and walks away, with tears on her face, from his burning body. Milkman, in *Song of Solomon*, abandons his cousin after a nineteen-year affair; she grieves herself to death. Son, in *Tar Baby*, drives his car through the bed in which his wife and her lover are sleeping. The quiet and passive Margaret Street systematically tortures her young son, Michael, with pin pricks. Sethe slits her baby's throat to keep the child from death in slavery. Fifty-five-year-old Joe Trace, in *Jazz*, shoots the eighteen-year-old woman whom he loves. Although these and other characters are never absolved of their guilt (they suffer the consequences of their criminality in one way or another), their crimes are mediated by the characters' humanity, by their desperate love and compassion. Bound by this paradox of human behavior—good people commit horrific acts—Morrison's people often embrace their transgressions and then transcend them. Not always, but sometimes, they may even be redeemed by the crime. Terry Otten, in his analysis of criminality in Morrison's work, perceives innocence to be worse than guilt. Otten correctly points out that in all of Morrison's novels "the fall from innocence becomes a necessary gesture of freedom and a profound act of self awareness."[14] Characters must make choices and suffer the outcome of those choices. Failing to choose is never an option for those who would be free. Sethe (*Beloved*) objectifies this dilemma when she asks why her brain refuses to shield her from the pain of knowing: "Why was there nothing it refused? No misery, no regret, no hateful picture too rotten to accept? Like a greedy child it snatched up everything. Just once, could it say, No thank You? I just ate and can't hold another bite?"[15] But Sethe's brain does consume much more, and when the pain spills over and erupts in violence against others, her tragic life elicits both sympathy and blame. Morrison's "moral vision," Otten surmises, "allows for few single-minded villains and heroes."[16]

It has been suggested that this generous judgment of moral exigencies reflects a premeditated revision of the black male literary tradition in which the world is divided into black/white, good/evil, virgin/whore, self/other, male/female paradigms. Most black women writers avoid such simplistic dichotomies; they avoid what critic Deborah McDowell calls "false choices."[17] *Sula,* McDowell points out, "is rife with liberating possibilities in that it transgresses all deterministic structures of opposition."[18] The shifting boundaries between good and evil in the novel are intentionally methodical, and this does not signal Morrison's "abdication of moral consciousness,"[19] but a revision of it—one that is truer to the complexity and indeterminacy of real life. In echoing this estimate of her work, Morrison says that she (and other black women) is writing to "repossess, rename, renown." She (and they) "look[s] at things in an unforgiving/loving way,"[20] a paradigm that is remarkable in its parallel to real life. This view accommodates contradictory responses and refuses simplistic, polarizing representations. Black women's texts, in America and the diaspora, Morrison notes, project a wide gaze. "It's not narrow, it's very probing and it does not flinch."[21]

Although Morrison flatly rejects a black feminist model of criticism or evaluation, she just as decisively asserts that she and other authors write for black women: "We are not addressing the men as some white female writers do. We are not attacking each other, as both black and white men do."[22] In fact, she recalls that when she began writing in the 1960s and 1970s there was a paucity of books about the black woman. There was no fiction representing her experience: "this person, this female, this black did not exist centre-self."[23]

The black woman, then, is an evolving presence in Morrison's work. Her first novel examines the consequences upon black womanhood of an oppressive standard of white beauty. The reader is called to witness the psychological disintegration of Pecola Breedlove, an adolescent girl whose blackness is an affront to a society in which blue eyes are valued above all others. In *Sula* Morrison moves from adolescence to womanhood, recording the community's response to one who dares to defy all narrowly conceived ideologies of woman. Only in defiance is freedom possible, the author suggests. Even in *Song of Solomon*, which is Morrison's only novel to be "driven by male characters,"[24] it is the presence of a woman, Pilate, which imparts the spiritual dimension for which the novel has been praised. Pilate, too, may be ancestor to the authentic women who haunt Jadine's dreams and challenge her choices in *Tar Baby*. Womanhood, motherhood, selfhood come together in *Beloved*, Morrison's novel about slavery's unspeakable crimes against a woman and a people. Sethe, like Pilate and Sula, refuses defeat even if triumph means violating conventional standards of moral behavior. In her latest novel, *Jazz*, Morrison asks what happens when women's dreams are deferred.

Woman's experience is not Morrison's sole concern, however. Her novels examine aspects of male life as well. She writes about the ways men dominate, sometimes ruthlessly, the ways some pursue freedom from responsibility to women and children, the ways others nurture family. Hers are certain kinds of men who, like all her characters, transcend sociological stereotypes and trample convention as they walk outside of societal norms. These, the author asserts, are the kind of "lawless" characters who interest her because they resist controls. "They make up their lives, or they find out who they are."[25] Morrison calls this spirit of adventure a masculine trait, but it is not found in men only; some women have it as well. Sula, according to Morrison, is "a masculine character in that sense. . . . She really behaves like a man. . . . She's adventuresome and will leave and try anything."[26]

Men and women, then, in Morrison's novels speculate; they take risks, and they seek. Her characters are often in motion. Sometimes the movement follows the historical migration of blacks out of slavery, out of the postwar South to the industrial North, or the movement may be in reverse from the North to the South. They walk, drive, take buses, fly, always in search of something—money, happiness, love, themselves. Yet, seldom is the object of their quest realized. More often than not the journey ends in isolation and alienation. They may find material success but never happiness. Only when the physical journey mirrors a psychological passage is the course even worthwhile. Morrison aims her characters "toward knowledge at the expense of happiness perhaps."[27] In *Song of Solomon*, Milkman Dead leaves his home in Michigan and flies to Pennsylvania in search of a cave with hidden gold. The gold, he thinks, will liberate him from any responsibility to family and community. He does not find gold, but he gains much more than wealth or financial independence. In Pennsylvania and later in Kentucky, he hears stories about his ancestors, stories about sacrifice and rebellion. This knowledge of the suffering and courage of those who came before empowers Milkman and propels him toward spiritual ascendence.

The right knowledge is important to Morrison's characters. They may be liberated by it. The things Milkman learns from his father in Michigan about proprietary control of money and people are useless, but the stories about his grandfather's and great-grandfather's resistance and defiance give him strength. These lessons in survival should not have to be learned late in life as they are by Milkman. They should come in childhood from "a chorus of mamas, grandmamas, aunts, cousins, sisters, neighbors, Sunday school teachers."[28] These are the people who comprise the community, which is central to Morrison's epistemology. Perhaps taking a cue from her own childhood experience in Lorain, Ohio, where the entire village assumed responsibility for a child's life, Morrison often calculates the psychological distance her characters have traveled by estimating their proximity to the community. The closer they are, the better. As the repository of self-affirming cultural traditions and beliefs, the community shapes character and gives a measure of protection from external assaults upon the psyche. Those who leave the village, Morrison says, must take it with them. "There is no need for the community if you have a sense of it inside."[29] Not internalizing it, however, invites tragedy. Hagar (*Song of Solomon*) remains uninitiated and beyond the boundaries of community fellowship. She therefore knows too little to save herself from insanity and death when she is abandoned by her lover. As one character asks, "Had anyone told her the things she ought to know . . . to give her the strength life demanded of her—and the humor with which to live it?"[30]

Some characters disdainfully reject the village and choose a different form of knowledge, and they too pay a price. Jadine (*Tar Baby*) is such a victim. She is orphaned in childhood and raised by an aunt and uncle in the household of their white employers. In this island of whiteness Jadine is far from any knowledge of village culture. Becoming a successful fashion model in Paris only widens this distance. Consequently, Jadine never feels authentic and complete. As an uninitiated black woman she will always be vulnerable to recriminations such as the accusing stare of an African woman she once encountered in a Paris supermarket.

Morrison's novels have a vital role to play in this process of acculturation. They cannot replace the village, but they can summon its spirit. Folk culture, as revealed in maxims, beliefs, attitudes, and ways of speaking, walking, and thinking, permeates Morrison's fiction and inspires its identifiably lyrical style. In her work mythic truths are revived, examined, and passed on, keeping the individual in touch with black American and African traditions. "I want to point out the dangers," Morrison writes, "to show that nice things don't always happen to the totally self-reliant if there is no conscious historical connection. To say, see—this is what will happen."[31] The future is threatening without knowledge and acceptance of the past.

As culturally specific as Morrison's novels are, they are not restrictive. They appeal to an eclectic audience, one that is not limited by race and gender. Hers are the themes of humanity: the quest for buried treasure, the fall from innocence, disconnection and alienation, the struggle for self-actualization. "We know thousands of these [clichés] in literature,"[32] Morrison points out. A bicultural reading of her novels by Karla Holloway and Stephanie Demetrakopoulos is a testimony to this universality in Morrison's work. Each of these critics reads Morrison from a different perspective, and each finds in Morrison a rich response to her academic and cultural experience. Demetrakopoulos explains:

> As a Black woman in a white society and institution (the university), Holloway brings many insights to the novels that I had not seen. Her studies of West African cultures as well as Black American culture also enlarge her critical approach so that her linguistic approach is philosophical, political, and anthropological.
> My academic background has been in Jungian and Women's Studies, so I am always looking for what is archetypically feminine, what is universal in feminine individuation. I also look for the spiritual in the female psyche. My use of Greek or Indian goddesses as a frame on characters in women's novels is for me a frame of universality that transcends my Judeo-Christian world. I am also interested in men's patterns of individuation and transitions from middle to old age, that I found plentifully in Morrison's generations of characters.[33]

Indeed, Morrison's fiction is a tour de force of American folk culture, but within its layers of mythic patterns, as Demetrakopoulos demonstrates, is also the archetypal experience of mankind and womankind.

Notes

1. Toni Morrison, "Lecture and Speech of Acceptance, Upon the Award of the Nobel Prize for Literature," *The Nobel Lecture in Literature* (New York: Alfred A. Knopf, 1994).

2. Nellie Y. McKay, "An Interview with Toni Morrison," *Contemporary Literature* 24 (Winter 1983): 413–29. Rpt. in *Toni Morrison: Critical Perspectives Past and Present,* ed. Henry Louis Gates, Jr., and K. A. Appiah (New York: Amistad, 1993) 407.

3. Toni Morrison, "Rootedness: The Ancestor as Foundation," *Black Women Writers (1950–1980),* ed. Marie Evans (New York: Doubleday, 1984) 344.

4. Morrison, "Rootedness" 345.

5. Morrison, "Rootedness" 345.

6. Morrison, "Rootedness" 345.

7. Morrison, "Rootedness" 340.

8. Thomas LeClair, "'The Language Must Not Sweat': A Conversation with Toni Morrison," *New Republic* 184 (21 March 1981): 26.

9. Trudier Harris, *Fiction and Folklore: The Novels of Toni Morrison* (Knoxville: University of Tennessee Press, 1991) 11.

10. Morrison, "Rootedness" 343.

11. Christina Davis, "Interview with Toni Morrison," *Presence Africaine* (First Quarterly, 1988). Rpt. in *Toni Morrison: Critical Perspectives Past and Present,* ed. Henry Louis Gates, Jr., and K. A. Appiah (New York: Amistad, 1993) 418–19.

12. Morrison, "Rootedness" 341.

13. Morrison, "Rootedness" 341.

14. Terry Otten, *The Crime of Innocence in the Fiction of Toni Morrison* (Columbia: University of Missouri Press, 1989) 5.

15. Toni Morrison, *Beloved* (New York: Alfred A. Knopf, 1987) 70.

16. Otten 96.

17. Deborah E. McDowell, "'The Self and the Other': Reading Toni Morrison's *Sula* and the Black Female Text," *Critical Essays on Toni Morrison,* ed. Nellie Y. McKay (Boston: G. K. Hall & Co., 1988) 80.

18. McDowell 79.

19. This phrase is borrowed from Robert Grant in "Absence into Presence: The Thematics of Memory and 'missing' Subjects in Toni Morrison's *Sula,*" *Critical Essays on Toni Morrison,* ed. Nellie Y. McKay (Boston: G. K. Hall & Co., 1988) 100.

20. Sandi Russell, "It's OK to Say OK," *Critical Essays on Toni Morrison,* ed. Nellie Y. McKay (Boston: G. K. Hall & Co., 1988) 46.

21. Davis 418.

22. Russell 46.

23. Russell 45.

24. Rosemarie K. Lester, "An Interview with Toni Morrison, Hessian Radio Network, Frankfurt, West Germany," *Critical Essays on Toni Morrison,* ed. Nellie Y. McKay (Boston: G. K. Hall & Co., 1988) 49.

25. Robert B. Stepto, "'Intimate Things in Place': A Conversation with Toni Morrison," *Massachusetts Review* 18 (Autumn 1977): 473–89. Rpt. in *Toni Morrison: Critical Perspectives Past and Present,* ed. Henry Louis Gates, Jr., and K. A. Appiah (New York: Amistad, 1993) 386.

26. Stepto 180.

27. McKay 406.

28. Toni Morrison, *Song of Solomon* (New York: Alfred A. Knopf, 1973) 311.

29. Russell 43.

30. Morrison, *Song of Solomon* 311.

31. Morrison, "Rootedness" 344.

32. Thomas LeClair, "Language" 26.

33. Karla F. C. Holloway and Stephanie A. Demetrakopoulos, *New Dimensions of Spirituality: A Biracial and Bicultural Reading of the Novels of Toni Morrison* (Westport, Conn.: Greenwood Press, 1987) 15–16.

2

BLACK GIRLHOOD
AND BLACK WOMANHOOD
THE BLUEST EYE AND SULA

From the beginning of her writing career Morrison has exercised a keen scrutiny of women's lives. *The Bluest Eye* and *Sula,* Morrison's first and second novels, are to varying extents about black girlhood and black womanhood, about women's connections to their families, their communities, to the larger social networks outside the community, to men, and to each other. Lending themselves to a reading as companion works, the novels complement one another thematically and may, in several ways, be viewed sequentially.[1] (Morrison calls her first four novels "evolutionary. One comes out of the other."[2] In *The Bluest Eye* she was "interested in talking about black girlhood," and in *Sula* she "wanted to move to the other part of their life." She wanted to ask, "what . . . do those feisty little girls grow up to be?")[3] *The Bluest Eye* directs a critical gaze at the process and symbols of imprinting the self during childhood and at what happens to the self when the process is askew and the symbols are defective. In *Sula,* Morrison builds on the knowledge gained in the first novel, revisits childhood, and then moves her characters and readers a step forward into women's struggles to change delimiting symbols and take control of their lives. But excavating an identity that has been long buried beneath stereotype and convention is a wrenching endeavor, and Morrison demonstrates in *Sula* that although recasting one's role in the community is possible, there is a price to be paid for change.

The Bluest Eye (1970)

The opening lines of *The Bluest Eye* incorporate two signifying aspects of Morrison's fiction. The first sentence, "Quiet as it's kept, there were no marigolds in the fall of 1941,"[4] emanates from the African-American community, capturing the milieu of "black women conversing with one another; telling a story, an anecdote, gossip[ing] about some one or event within the circle, the family, the neighborhood."[5] The line also demonstrates Morrison's urge to connect with her reader by choosing "speakerly" phrasing that has a "back fence connotation." Morrison explains:

> The intimacy I was aiming for, the intimacy between the reader and the page, could start up immediately because the secret is being shared at best, and eavesdropped upon, at the least. Sudden familiarity or instant intimacy seemed crucial to me then, writing my first novel. I did not want the reader to have time to wonder "what do I have to do, to give up, in order to read this? What defense do I need, what distance maintain?" Because I know (and the reader does not—he or she has to wait for the second sentence) that this is a terrible story about things one would rather not know anything about.[6]

The line's foreboding aura charitably prepares the reader for powerful truths soon to be revealed. The pervading absence of flowers in 1941 sets that year off from all others and produces a prophetic and ominous quality which unfolds in the second line: "We thought, at the time, that it was because Pecola was having her father's baby that the marigolds did not grow" (3). Exploiting the child speaker's naive but poignant logic, Morrison requires the reader, during this first encounter, to be accountable, to acknowledge a dreadful deed and respond to its dreadful consequences. "If the conspiracy that the opening words announce is entered into by the reader," Morrison explains, "then the book can be seen to open with its close: a speculation on the disruption of 'nature' as being a social disruption with tragic individual consequences in which the reader, as part of the population of the text, is implicated."[7] This three-way collaboration between author, speaker, and reader is the effect for which Morrison strives in all her novels.

From this profoundly stirring beginning Morrison advances to an equally moving examination of Pecola's life—her unloving childhood, her repudiation by nearly everyone she encounters, and finally the complete disintegration of self. Through it all Morrison exposes and indicts those who promulgate standards of beauty and behavior that devalue Pecola's sensitivities and contribute to her marginalized existence.

The search for culprits is not arduous. The storekeeper who sells Mary Jane candies to Pecola avoids touching her hand when she pays and barely disguises his contempt for her: "She looks up at him and sees the vacuum where curiosity ought to lodge. . . . The total absence of human recognition—the glazed separateness. . . . It has an edge; somewhere in the bottom lid is the distaste. . . . The distaste must be for her, her blackness . . . and it is the blackness that accounts for, that creates, the vacuum edged with distance in white eyes" (36–37). The white Yacobowski is condemned for his cultural blindness, but he is not the only one responsible for Pecola's pain. Responsibility must be shared by blacks who assuage their own insults from society by oppressing those like Pecola who are vulnerable. Little black boys jeer and taunt her with "Black e mo. Black e mo. Yadaddsleepsnekked" (50), defensively ignoring the color of their own skins. But "it was their contempt for their own blackness that gave the first insult its teeth. They seem to have taken all of their smoothly cultivated ignorance, their exquisitely learned self-hatred, their elaborately designed hopelessness and sucked it all up into a fiery cone of scorn that had burned for ages in the hollows of their minds . . ." (50).

Teachers ignore Pecola in the classroom, giving their attention instead to a "high-yellow dream child with long brown hair" (47) and "sloe green eyes" (48). And when this same high-yellow Maureen Peal declares to Pecola and the MacTeer sisters "I *am* cute! And you ugly! Black and ugly black e mos" (56), she is dangerously affirming intraracial acceptance of the world's denigration of blackness. "Respectable," "milk-brown" women like Geraldine see Pecola's torn dress and uncombed hair and are confronted with the blackness they have spent lifetimes rejecting. For Morrison these women are antithetical to the village culture she respects. They attend to the "careful development of thrift, patience, high morals and good manners" (64) as these are defined by white society. And they fear "the dreadful funkiness of passion, the funkiness of nature, the funkiness of the wide range of human emotions" (64) because these qualities are defined by black society. They are shamed by the "laugh that is too loud, the enunciation a little too round; the gesture a little too generous. They hold their behind in for fear of a sway too free; when they wear lipstick, they never cover the entire mouth for fear of lips too thick, and they worry, worry, worry about the edges of their hair" (64). As one of these women, Geraldine executes the tyranny of standardized beauty that enthralls some in the black community and terrorizes too many others.

When Pecola stands in Geraldine's house—tricked there by Geraldine's hateful son—she transgresses a line demarking "colored people" from "niggers," light-skinned from dark, hand-me-down whiteness from genuine culture. In her innocence Pecola does not perceive the transgression or its consequences. To her, Geraldine's world and house are beautiful. The house's ordered prettiness sharply contrasts the shabby makedo appearance of the Breedloves' storefront. Geraldine, however, does perceive Pecola's outrageous breech, and the hurting child that Pecola is becomes a "nasty little black bitch" (72) in Geraldine's mouth. Geraldine sets her teeth against any recognition of some part of who she is in Pecola. To Pecola, Geraldine is "the pretty milk-brown lady in the pretty gold and green house" (72). To Morrison, she is a shadow image of the Dick-and-Jane life, a sadistic approximation of the storybook people. Through her Morrison demonstrates that such a life as Geraldine's is only validated by exclusion of others.

Michael Awkward discusses this "purgative abuse" of Pecola in terms of the black community's guilt about its own inability to measure up to some external ideal of beauty and behavior. Pecola objectifies this failure (which results in self-hatred) and must be purged. She becomes the black community's shadow of evil (even as the black community is the white community's evil). "In combating the shadow . . . the group is able to rid itself ceremonially of the veil that exists within both the individual member and the community at large. To be fully successful, such exorcism requires a visibly imperfect, shadow-consumed scapegoat" like Pecola.[8]

Even her parents, Cholly and Pauline Breedlove, relate to Pecola in this way. Ironically named since they breed not love but violence and misery, Cholly and Pauline eventually destroy their daughter, whose victimization is a bold symbol of their own despair and frustrations. In the pathos of their defeated lives, Morrison demonstrates the process by which self-hatred becomes scapegoating.

Pauline's lame foot makes her pitiable and invisible until she marries Cholly. But pleasure in marriage lasts only until she moves from Kentucky to Ohio and confronts northern standards of physical beauty and style. She is despised by snooty black women who snicker at her lameness, her unstraightened hair, and her provincial speech. In the movie theaters she seeks relief from these shortcomings through daydreams of Clark Gable and Jean Harlow. But even in high heels, makeup, and a Harlow hairstyle Pauline is a failure. "In equating physical beauty with virtue, she stripped her mind, bound it, and collected self-contempt by the heap," (95) which she deposits on her husband and children who fail by "the scale of absolute beauty . . . she absorbed in full from the silver screen" (95). Eventually, Pauline gives up on her own family and takes refuge in the soft beauty surrounding her in the Fisher home, where she works—the crisp linens, white towels, the little Fisher girl's yellow hair. She cannot afford such beauty and style. In the Fisher house, however, she has dominion over creditors and service people "who humiliated her when she went to them on her own behalf [but] respected her, were even intimidated by her, when she spoke for the Fishers" (101). With the Fishers she had what she could not have at home—"power, praise, and luxury" (99). By the time Pecola finds herself awkwardly standing in the Fisher's kitchen, responsible for the spilled remains of a freshly baked pie at her feet, Pauline is incapable of a mother's love and forgiveness. Her best response is knocking Pecola to the floor and running to console the crying Fisher child.

In substituting fierce intolerance of her family for love, Pauline refuses what she cannot transform. Her husband is an irresponsible drunk; the son and daughter are sloven. Only she has order and beauty and only in the Fisher house. Under these conditions Pauline is reborn as self-righteous martyr with no time for movies, unfulfilled dreams, and foolish notions of romantic love. "All the meaningfulness of her life was in her work. . . . She was an active church woman . . . defended herself mightily against Cholly . . . and felt she was fulfilling a mother's role conscientiously when she pointed out their father's faults to keep them from having them, or punished them when they showed any slovenliness, no matter how slight, when she worked twelve to sixteen hours a day to support them" (100).

Like Pauline, Cholly too is driven by personal demons which he attempts to purge in violence against his family. Pauline does not see or understand Cholly's hurts, but Morrison represents them as remarkably egregious. Callously abandoned on a garbage dump by his mother, years later Cholly searches for the father who also discards him. His response to his father's angry denunciations—crying and soiling his pants—eclipses any opportunity for emotional maturity and returns him, in a sense, to the helplessness of his abandonment in infancy. After the rejection, in a nearby river he seeks relief, even rebirth, curled for hours in the fetal position with fists in eyes. For a while he finds consolation in "the dark, the warmth, the quiet . . . [engulfing him] like the skin and flesh of an elderberry protecting its own seed" (124). Protection is short-lived, however. There is no prelapsarian innocence available to Cholly.

In marrying Pauline, Cholly seems fully recovered from these earlier traumas. Initially, he is kind, compassionate, protective, but these feelings too are fleeting. He retreats from her emotional dependence, he is humiliated by economic powerlessness, and he mitigates his frustrations in drink and abuse. In turning on Pauline, Cholly fights whom he can and not whom he should. This is the lesson of childhood learned when he is forced by armed white men who discover him with Darlene in the woods to continue his first act of sexual intimacy while they watch and ridicule. When the men leave in search of other prey, Cholly realizes that hating them is futile, and he decides instead to hate Darlene for witnessing his degradation. He could not protect her so he settles for despising her. Later Pauline comes to stand for Darlene in Cholly's mind: "He poured out on her the sum of all his inarticulate fury and aborted desires" (37). Cholly, then, needs Pauline to objectify his failure.

His treatment of Pecola may also be seen in terms of scapegoating but not entirely. While Pecola's ugliness is an affront to Pauline's surreptitious creation of beauty in the Fisher house, it is a sad reminder to Cholly of not only his unhappiness but Pecola's as well. Such concern makes him a somewhat sympathetic character. He is one of Morrison's traveling men, one whose freedom to do as he pleases is jeopardized by dependent, possessive women. He has roamed around dangerously, carelessly, irresponsibly, lovingly. The appealing contradiction of his life could find expression only in black music. "Only a musician would sense, know, without even knowing that he knew, Cholly was free. Dangerously free" (125). After his mother's abandonment and his father's rejection, Cholly has little to loose, and his behavior is disdainful of consequences. "It was in this godlike state that he met Pauline Williams," (126) and marriage to her threatens to conquer him.

In romanticizing Cholly, Morrison defies the unflattering orthodoxy of black maleness and makes peace with the conflict between responsibility to family and freedom to leave. Morrison respects the freedom even as she embraces the responsibility. In the freedom she sees "tremendous possibility for masculinity among black men."[9] Sometimes such men are unemployed or in prison, but they have a spirit of adventure and a deep complexity that interests Morrison. No doubt she views their freedom as a residue of the "incredible . . . magic and feistiness in black men that nobody has been able to wipe out."[10] Cholly exercises his freedom, but not before he commits a heinous crime against Pecola. Even his crime, however, is tempered by the author's compassion for Cholly. Coming home drunk and full of self-pity, Cholly sees Pecola and is overcome with love and regret that he has nothing to relieve her hopelessness. "Guilt and impotence rose in a bilious duct. What could he do for her—ever? What give her? What say to her? What could a burned-out black man say to the hunched back of his eleven-year-old daughter?" (127). His answer is rape—in spite of himself. In rendering this incomprehensible instance, Morrison captures the curious mixture of hate and tenderness that consumes Cholly. "The hatred would not let him pick her up" when the violation is over; "the tenderness forced him to cover her" (129). The awful irony of his position is overwhelming. In the end Cholly's complexity dominates the moment. Having never been parented, "he could not even comprehend what such a relationship should be" (126). And being dangerously free, he has no restraints.

Morrison does have sympathy for Cholly (she admits that she connects "Cholly's 'rape' by the white men to his own of his daughter"[11]), but he is not absolved; he dies soon after in a workhouse. And Morrison does not minimize his crime against his daughter. Pecola's childlike "stunned silence," "the tightness of her vagina," the painfully "gigantic thrust," her "fingers clinching," her "shocked body," and finally her unconsciousness bear witness to Morrison's aim in the novel to represent Pecola's perspective, to translate her heartbreak. "This most masculine act of aggression becomes feminized in my language," Morrison says. It is "passive," she continues, "and, I think, more accurately repellent when deprived of the male 'glamor of shame' rape is (or once was) routinely given."[12]

Feminizing language does not lead Morrison to comfortable binary oppositions of good and evil, feminine and masculine. Rather, it leads to a sensitive treatment of the complex emotions that determine character, male and female. In Morrison's writing there are no easy villains to hate; there are no predictable behaviors.

Just as Cholly is not as reprehensible as he might be, Pauline is not as sympathetic as she might be if she were stereotypically portrayed as an abused wife and as a mother. In fact, Pauline in some sense is as culpable as Cholly for Pecola's suffering. Cholly's love is corrupt and tainted, but Pauline is unloving. After the rape Morrison subtly alludes to the difference: "So when the child regained consciousness, she was lying on the kitchen floor under a heavy quilt, trying to connect the pain between her legs with the face of her mother looming over her" (129). Is Pauline associated with the pain? She did not physically rape Pecola, but she has ravaged the child's self-worth and left her vulnerable to assaults of various proportions.

With single-minded determination Pauline survives, but Pecola withdraws into the refuge of insanity. Like the dandelions whose familiar yellow heads she thinks are pretty, Pecola is poisoned by rejection. But unlike the dandelions, she does not have the strength to persist, and in madness she simply substitutes her inchoate reality with a better one: she has blue eyes which everyone admires and envies. In pathetic conversations with an imaginary friend, Pecola repeatedly elicits confirmation that hers are "the bluest eyes in the whole world" (161), that they are "much prettier than the sky. Prettier than Alice-and-Jerry Storybook eyes" (159).

Pecola's sad fantasy expresses Morrison's strongest criticism of a white standard of beauty that excludes most black women and that destroys those who strive to measure up but cannot. Everywhere there are reminders of this failure: the coveted blond-haired, blue-eyed dolls that arrive at Christmas, Shirley Temple movies, high-yellow dream children like Maureen Peal. And for Pecola the smiling white face of little Mary Jane on the candy wrapper, "blond hair in gentle disarray, blue eyes looking at her out of a world of clean comfort" (38). In desperation Pecola believes that nothing bad could be viewed by such eyes. Cholly and Mrs. Breedlove (Pecola's name for her mother) would not fight; her teachers and classmates would not despise her; she would be safe. And, ironically, perhaps Pecola is right. With the blue eyes of her distorted reality comes the awful safety of oblivion.

Pecola's tragedy exposes the fallacy of happily-ever-after storybook life. Morrison repeatedly calls attention to this falseness. In the prologue and chapter headings are recounted the elementary story of Dick and Jane, mother and father:

Here is the house. It is green and white. It has a red door. It is very pretty. Here is the family. Mother, Father, Dick, and Jane live in the green-and-white house. They are very happy. See Jane. She has a red dress. She wants to play. Who will play with Jane? See the cat. It goes meow-meow. Come and play. Come play with Jane. The kitten will not play. See Mother. Mother is very nice. Mother, will you play with Jane? Mother laughs. Laugh, Mother, laugh. See Father. He is big and strong. Father, will you play with Jane? Father is smiling. Smile, Father, smile. See the dog. Bowwow goes the dog. Do you want to play with Jane? See the dog run. Run, dog, run. Look, look. Here comes a friend. The friend will play with Jane. They will play a good game. Play, Jane, play. (1)

In two subsequent versions Morrison distorts the Dick-and-Jane text. In bold print with no spacing between words, these latter passages take on a frenetic tone that signals perversion of communal perfection for Morrison's characters, who do not blithely run and play and live happily ever after. In removing standard grammatical codes, symbols of Western culture, Morrison expurgates the white text as she constructs the black. Timothy Bell aptly points out that "Morrison is literally deconstructing the essential white text, removing capitalizations, punctuation, and finally the spacing until the white text is nothing more than a fragmentation of its former self at the beginning of the chapter."[13] Home for Pecola is not the green and white picture-perfect house of white myth. Home is a storefront where mother and father curse and fight, brother runs away from home, and sister wishes with all her soul for blue eyes. Pecola appropriates the storybook version of life because her own is too gruesome. In her life she is subject to other people's cruel whims to which she can offer no voice of protest.

Indeed, she has no voice in this text at all, a condition which loudly echoes her entire existence. She has no control over the events in her life and no authority over the narrative of those events. That authority goes to twelve-year-old Claudia, who narrates major portions of Pecola's story with compassion and understanding. Claudia and her older sister Frieda are the "we" of the opening paragraph. They witness Pecola's despair and try to save her. "Her pain agonized me," Claudia says, "I wanted to open her up, crisp her edges, ram a stick down that hunched and curving spine, force her to stand erect and spit the misery out on the streets" (61). But the sisters fail. They do not save Pecola from her breakup. As the girls mourn their failure, Morrison chronicles the loss of their innocence. But unlike Pecola's short-circuited innocence, their loss is part of a natural ritual of growing up.

Morrison proffers Claudia and Frieda as foils to Pecola. They are strong and sturdy; Pecola is not. Claudia's independence and confidence especially throw Pecola's helplessness into stark relief. For Claudia, blue-eyed dolls at Christmas and Shirley Temple dancing with Bojangles Robinson are unappealing and even insulting. With youthful but penetrating insight, she declares her exemption from "the universal love of white dolls, Shirley Temples, and Maureen Peals" (148).

Claudia and her sister traverse Morrison's landscape of black girlhood. Bound by a social environment that is hostile to their kind, they have "become headstrong, devious and arrogant" (150) enough to dismiss limitations and believe that they can "change the course of events and alter a human life" (150). With ingenious faith in themselves, Claudia and Frieda attempt to rescue Pecola and her baby. They would make beauty where only ugliness resided by planting marigolds deep in the earth and receiving the magic of their beauty as a sign of Pecola's salvation. When neither marigolds nor Pecola survive, the girls blame a community that is seduced by a white standard of beauty and that makes Pecola its scapegoat: "All of us—all who knew her—felt so wholesome after we cleaned ourselves on her. We were beautiful when we stood astride her ugliness. . . . We honed our egos on her, padded our characters with her frailty, and yawned in the fantasy of our strength" (160).

For the most part their parents, Mr. and Mrs. MacTeer, save Claudia and Frieda from this sort of persecution. Mr. MacTeer (unlike Cholly) acts as a father should in protecting his daughter from a lecherous boarder. Mrs. MacTeer's place is not in a white family's kitchen, but in her own, where familiar smells hold sway and where her singing about "hard times, bad times and somebody-done-gone-and-left-me times" (28) proclaims that pain is endurable, even sweet. To her daughters she bequeaths a legacy of compassion for others and defiance in the face of opposition. Her love for them was "thick and dark as Alaga syrup" (7). The MacTeers embody the communal resiliency at the heart of black culture.

Mrs. MacTeer is not one of Morrison's ancestors—a person wise in the ways of life who transmits that wisdom and knowledge of self to the uninitiated. She is, however, one of Morrison's nurturers. Claudia remembers the feel of her mother's hands on her forehead and chest when she is sick: "I think," she says, "of somebody with hands who does not want me to die" (7). Mrs. MacTeer takes Pecola in when Cholly burns his family out. She presides over Pecola's first menses, hugging her reassuringly (the only hug the adolescent Pecola ever receives; Mrs. Breedlove's hugs and assurances are reserved for the little Fisher girl). But Mrs. MacTeer's influence in Pecola's life is short in duration. With no one else available Pecola turns to the whores who live upstairs over the storefront for instruction given lovingly. China, Marie, and Poland stand in opposition to the Geraldines in the community. They are not pretentious heirs to false puritanical values, and Morrison respects their unvarnished natures. "Three merry gargoyles. Three merry harridans," they are quick to laugh or sing. Defying all stereotypes of pitiable women gone wrong, they make no apologies for themselves and seek no sympathy. "They were not young girls in whores' clothing, or whores regretting their loss of innocence. They were whores in whores' clothes, whores who had never been young and had no word for innocence" (43). Pecola loves these women, and they are more than willing to share the lessons they've learned, but their lessons are wrong for Pecola. They can tell her stories that are breezy and rough about lawless men and audacious women. But they cannot teach her what she wants most to know: how to be loved by a mother and father, by a community, and by a society. For that she turns in the end to Soaphead Church, the itinerant spiritualist and flawed human being. A pedophile and con man, Soaphead has not transcended the pain of life's humiliations and is deeply scarred. Morrison describes him as "that kind of black"[14] for whom blackness is a burden to be borne with self-righteous indignation. Of West Indian and colonial English ancestry that has long been in social decline, Soaphead, existing at the bottom of the descent, is "wholly convinced that if black people were more like white people they would be better off."[15] He, therefore, appreciates Pecola's yearning for blue eyes. But Soaphead's powers are fraudulent as are his claims to have helped Pecola by "giving" her blue eyes; he does little more than use her in his own schemes of revenge against God and man. With no one to help her counteract the love of white dolls with blue eyes, Pecola cannot help herself, and she is obliged to be the victim—always.

Indeed the effects of Pecola's devastation are unrelenting as measured in the passing of time in the novel—season after season: Morrison names each of the novel's sections after a season of the year, beginning with autumn and ending with summer. The headings are ironically prophetic preludes to the story segments. They stand out as perverse contradictions of Pecola's experiences: thematic progression is not from dormancy to rebirth as the autumn to spring movement would suggest. There is no renewal for Pecola. In spring she is violated; by summer she is annihilated. Morrison uses this disruption of nature to signal the cosmic proportion of Pecola's injury.

Sula (1973)

The Bluest Eye was not commercially successful at the time of its publication (its popularity has risen in tandem with Morrison's reputation). Yet, it did inaugurate its author's public literary life. After writing it, Morrison became a frequent reviewer in the *New York Times* and an authoritative commentator on black culture and women's concerns. Three years later *Sula* was both a commercial and critical triumph. It was excerpted in *Redbook* and widely reviewed. The Book-of-the-Month Club selected it as an alternate, and in 1975 it was nominated for the National Book Award.

If *The Bluest Eye* chronicles to some extent an annihilation of self, *Sula*, on the contrary, validates resiliency in the human spirit and celebrates the self. In *Sula* Morrison returns to the concerns of girlhood explored in her first novel, but this time she approaches her subject in celebration, as if to see what miracles love and friendship may accomplish for Sula and Nel that they could not for Pecola, Claudia, and Frieda.

Sula Peace and Nel Wright are each the only daughter of mothers whose distance leaves the young girls alone with dreams of someone to erase the solitude. When they first met, "they felt the ease and comfort of old friends."[16] Indeed "their meeting was fortunate, for it let them use each other to grow on" (44). Sula's spontaneous intensity is relieved by Nel's passive reserve. Sula loves the ordered neatness of Nel's home and her life, and Nel likes Sula's "household of throbbing disorder constantly awry with things, people, voices and the slamming of doors . . ." (44). Over the years "they found relief in each other's personality" (45).

In examining their friendship, Morrison tests its endurance. As she says, not much had been done with women as friends; men's relationships are often the subject of fiction, but what about women's strongest bonds? As perfect complements, one incomplete without the other, Sula and Nel together face life, death, and marriage, and eventually they also must face separation. Throughout, Morrison affirms the necessity of their collaboration.

Adolescence for Nel and Sula is marked not by individuation, but by merger, as a single, provocative play scene illustrates. In the summer of their twelfth year, with thoughts of boys and with "their small breasts just now beginning to create some pleasant discomfort when they were lying on their stomachs" (49), the girls escape to the park. In silence and without looking at each other, they begin to play in the grass, stroking the blades. "Nel found a thick twig and, with her thumbnail, pulled away its bark until it was stripped to a smooth, creamy innocence" (49). Sula does the same. Soon they begin poking "rhythmically and intensely into the earth," making small neat holes. "Nel began a more strenuous digging and, rising to her knee, was careful to scoop out the dirt as she made her hole deeper. Together they worked until the two holes were one and the same" (50). In their symbolic sexual play, Nel and Sula, unlike Pecola, have absolute control in this necessary right of passage (without the intrusion of a masculine presence) which conjoins them until, like the holes, they are one and the same.

Two other significant moments define their intimacy as well. The first is Sula's cutting off the tip of her finger in response to a threat by a group of white boys whose menacing bodies block the girl's route home. If she could do that to herself, what would she do to them, Sula asks the shocked boys. The second is the death of Chicken Little, the little boy whose body Sula swings around and around in play until her hands slip, and he flies out over the river and drowns. Nel watches, and no one discovers their culpability. At the graveside they hold hands. "At first, as they stood there, their hands were clenched together. They relaxed slowly until during the walk back home their fingers were laced in as gentle a clasp as that of any two young girlfriends trotting up the road on a summer day wondering what happened to butterflies in the winter" (56–57).

Not even Nel's marriage dissolves their "friendship [that] was so close, they themselves had difficulty distinguishing one's thoughts from the other's" (72). They are both happy; Nel becomes a wife, and Sula goes to college. Ten years later Sula's return imparts a magic to Nel's days that marriage had not. "Her old friend had come home. . . . Sula, whose past she had lived through and with whom the present was a constant sharing of perceptions. Talking to Sula had always been a conversation with herself" (82). Their lives resume an easy rhythm until Nel walks into her bedroom and finds her husband and Sula naked. Not surprisingly, this episode supersedes the women's friendship. Jude leaves town, Nel, and their children, and Nel blames Sula. Three years later, when Nel visits a dying Sula, she asks, "Why you didn't love me enough to leave him alone. To let him love me. You had to take him away" (125). Sula replies, "What you mean take him away? . . . If we were such good friends, how come you couldn't get over it?" (125).

With Sula's question Morrison calls into doubt the primacy of Nel's marriage over the women's friendship, intimating that their friendship may even supplant the marriage. Years after Sula's death, Nel comes to this realization at her friend's grave. "All that time, all that time, I thought I was missing Jude. . . . We was girls together. . . . O Lord, Sula . . . girl, girl, girlgirlgirl" (149).

Nel and Sula's estrangement offers Morrison an opportunity to examine women's lives in and out of marriage. As girls Nel and Sula had cunningly authored the dimensions of their own existence without the permission or approval of their families or the community. "Because each had discovered years before that they were neither white nor male and that all freedom and triumph was forbidden to them, they had set about creating something else to be" (44). Morrison does not elaborate further on the specific nature of their creation, but clearly each positions herself just outside the village perspective, thinking and behaving with a certain independence. "In the safe harbor of each other's company they could afford to abandon the ways of other people and concentrate on their own perceptions of things" (47).

The experience that determines Nel's perspective is a train ride with her mother. The two travel for days from Ohio to New Orleans for Nel's great-grandmother's funeral. Her mother's shuffling acquiescence in the face of the white conductor's hostility during the trip, the sullen black male passengers whose refusal to help her mother reflects their own helpless humiliation, the indignity of squatting to relieve themselves in the brush in full view of the train, her mother's stiff shame of her own creole mother's life as a prostitute—all these experiences teach Nel lessons about other people's vulnerabilities. Back home in the safety of her bedroom she resolves to develop her strengths. Looking in the mirror, she whispers to herself "I'm me. . . . I'm me. I'm not their daughter. I'm not Nel. I'm me. Me . . ." (24). Adopting me-ness as her mantra, Nel gathers power and joy, and the "strength to cultivate a friend [Sula] in spite of her mother" (25). Nel's daring is eclipsed, however, by marriage to Jude. For Helene Wright, Nel's mother, marriage is one of the neat conditions of living that defines a woman's place, and Nel accepts a similar arrangement for herself. Nel does not choose Jude; she accepts his choosing her as a way of completing himself. Without Nel, Jude is an enraged "waiter hanging around a kitchen like a woman" (71) because bigotry keeps him from doing better. "With her he was head of a household pinned to an unsatisfactory job out of necessity. The two of them together would make one Jude" (71). In marrying Jude, Nel gives up her youthful dreams (before she met Sula) of being "wonderful" and of "trips she would take, alone . . . to faraway places" (25). In marrying Jude, she gives up her me-ness.

Predictably, when Jude leaves, after his betrayal with Sula, Nel suffers psychic disintegration, and later, after a necessary recovery, she endures shrinkage of the self. She considers the release that may come with death, but that will have to wait because she has three children to raise. In this condition Nel wraps herself in the conventional mantle of sacrifice and martyrdom and takes her place with the rest of the women in the community. Although Nel does not discover it until after Sula's death and she is old, the real loss in her life is that of Sula and not Jude. And the real tragedy is that she has allowed herself to become less than she was.

Sula is different from Nel. It is Sula's rebellious spirit that fuels the intermittent moments of originality that Nel manages to have. In Sula's presence Nel has "sparkle or sputter" (618). Sula resists any authority or controls, and Morrison offers her as one of the lawless individuals whose life she is so fond of examining. From Sula's days in childhood when she retreated to the attic, she rebels against conventionality. She is surprised and saddened by Nel's rejection of her over Jude. She had not expected Nel to behave "the way the others would have" (635). But nothing, not even her closest and only friend's censures will force Sula to abridge herself.

Even near death Sula will have none of Nel's limitations. To the end she proclaims, "I sure did live in this world. . . . I got my mind. And what goes on in it. Which is to say, I got me" (645). Sula's me-ness remains intact; she has not betrayed herself as Nel has, and any loneliness she feels is a price she is willing to pay for freedom.

By and large, Sula's assessment of her past is credible. Only once has she come close to subsuming herself to some other, named Ajax. Shortly after Ajax shows up at her door with a quart of milk tucked under each arm, Sula begins to think of settling down with him. All of the men in her past had, over the years, "merged into one large personality" (104) of sameness. "She had been looking . . . for a friend, and it took her a while to discover that a lover was not a comrade and could never be—for a woman" (104). But those thoughts exist before she meets Ajax; he is different in some ways. He brings her beautiful and impractical gifts: "clusters of black berries still on their branches, four meal-fried porgies wrapped in a salmon-colored sheet of the Pittsburgh *Courier,* a handful of jacks, two boxes of lime Jell-Well, a hunk of ice-wagon ice . . ." (104). Sula is most interested in him, however, because he talks to her and is never condescending in conversation. "His refusal to baby or protect her, his assumption that she was both tough and wise—all that coupled with a wide generosity of spirit . . . sustained Sula's interest and enthusiasm" (110).

Their interlude ends when Ajax discovers Sula's possessiveness. For the first time Sula wants to be responsible for a man and to protect him from the dangers of life. Giving in to a nesting instinct that is new for her, she is on the verge of making his life her own. But before that happens Ajax leaves, and Sula has only his driver's license as proof of his ever having been there. Sula's sorrow is intense, but short-lived, unlike Nel's enduring suffering for Jude. In the end, when Nel accuses her of never being able to keep a man, Sula counters that she would never waste life trying to keep a man: "They ain't worth more than me. And besides, I never loved no man because he was worth it. Worth didn't have nothing to do with it. . . . My mind did. That's all" (124). Sula had needed Nel, but she had never needed a man to extend herself. Even in lovemaking she had manufactured her own satisfaction, "in the postcoital privateness in which she met herself, welcomed herself, and joined herself in matchless harmony" (107). With Ajax those private moments had not been necessary, but without him Sula abides. The self, Morrison instructs, should not be liable in its own betrayal.

Sula is, without doubt, a manifesto of freedom, and that fact in large part accounts for its popularity with readers and critics who champion its triumphant chronicle of a black woman's heroism. That does not mean, however, that the novel approximates the ideal or that Sula's character is not flawed. Morrison describes her as an artist without a medium. "Her strangeness . . . was the consequence of an idle imagination. Had she paints, or clay, or knew the discipline of the dance, or strings; had she anything to engage her tremendous curiosity and her gift for metaphor, she might have exchanged the restlessness and preoccupation with whim for an activity that provided her with all she yearned for" (105). An art form augments life by giving it purpose; perhaps it teaches the individual compassion, but without it someone like Sula is, as Morrison describes her, strange, naive, and dangerous.

In this view Sula is without an essential quality of humanity. She has taken little from others, but more important she has *given* little.[17] She does not mean others harm: "She had no thought at all of causing Nel pain when she bedded down with Jude" (103), but without the moderating and mediating influence of her own humanity, Sula is unthinking and childlike. It is as if some crucial element of consciousness had been arrested in childhood when she overheard her mother say to a friend that she loved Sula but did not like her or when "her major feeling of responsibility [for Chicken Little's death] had been exorcised" (102). After that, "she had no center, no speck around which to grow" (103). The most bizarre episodes of her conduct may be understood in this context: feeling no emotion but curiosity while watching her mother burn to death, putting her grandmother in a nursing home for no good reason, and, of course, having sex with her best friend's husband.

Imperfect as she is, however, Sula does escape the falseness and emptiness of Nel's life. As Nel takes her place beside the other women in the community, she and they are identified with spiders, whose limitations keep them dangling "in the dark dry places . . . terrified of the free fall" (104). And if they do fall, they envision themselves as victims of someone else's evil. Sula, on the other hand, is one of Morrison's characters who is associated with flight, the metaphor for freedom. Sula is not afraid to use her wings fully to "surrender to the downward flight" (104). She is unafraid of the free fall.

Flight in Morrison is usually associated with men and not with women, who are more often than not Morrison's nurturers. Of course, Morrison offers neither quality by itself as the archetypal model; in the best scenarios the individual is capable of both nurturance and flight. Indeed, Nel and Sula are incomplete without each other. As Morrison says, "Nel knows and believes in all the laws of that community. She *is* the community. She believes in its values. Sula does not. She does not believe in any of those laws and breaks them all. Or ignores them."[18] But both positions are problematic, Morrison continues: "Nel does not make that 'leap'—she doesn't know about herself [she does not discover until too late, for example that she had watched Chicken Little's drowning with excitement]. . . . Sula, on the other hand, knows all there is to know about herself. . . . But she has trouble making a connection with other people and just feeling that lovely sense of accomplishment of being close in a very strong way."[19] Nurturance without invention and imagination is analogous to flight without responsibility. Ajax is the only other character in the novel who is identified with flying. He loves airplanes, and he thinks often of airplanes, pilots, "and the deep sky that held them both" (109). When he takes long trips to big cities, other people imagine him pursuing some exotic fun that is unavailable to them; in truth, he is indulging his obsession with flying by standing around airports watching planes take off.

Metaphorically, Ajax is always in flight—from conventionality. Without work, but willing to be responsible for himself, Ajax does not take cover in domesticity. Unlike Jude, who is only half a man without Nel as his refuge from life's injustices, Ajax does not need Sula to kiss his hurts and make them better. Unlike Jude, Ajax has self-esteem that is not diminished by white men's refusal of work, and unlike Jude, he does not run away and leave behind a wife and children. Ajax does leave Sula, but his action is not a betrayal. Ajax and Sula had come together, not as fractional individuals in need of the other to be complete, but as whole people, and when that equation is threatened by Sula's possessiveness, Ajax leaves for Dayton and airplanes. Of men like Ajax Morrison writes:

> They are the misunderstood people in the world. There's a wildness that they have, a nice wildness. It has bad effects in a society such as the one in which we live. It's pre-Christ in the best sense. It's Eve. When I see this

wildness gone in a person, it's sad. This special lack of restraint, which is a part of human life and is best typified in certain black males, is of particular interest to me. . . . Everybody knows who "that man" is, and they may give him bad names and call him a "street nigger"; but when you take away the vocabulary of denigration, what you have is somebody who is fearless and who is comfortable with that fearlessness. It's not about meanness. It's a kind of self-flagellant resistance to certain kinds of control, which is fascinating. Opposed to accepted notions of progress, the lock step life, they live in the world unreconstructed and that's it.[20]

As characters in flight both Ajax and Sula stand in opposition to the community that is firmly rooted in ritual and tradition. As the devoted son of "an evil conjure woman" (109), whom most regarded as a neglectful mother, Ajax is accustomed to rebuffing public opinion, and as a man he is given a license to do so. As a woman Sula must *take* that license, and in the fray she alienates the community. Sula returns to town after ten years and refuses to honor the town's ceremonies: "She came to their church suppers without underwear, bought their steaming platters of food and merely picked at it—relishing nothing, exclaiming over no one's ribs or cobbler. They believed that she was laughing at their God" (99). Soon the town names her a devil and prepares to live with its discovery. In fact, Morrison says, the town's toleration of Sula is in some way a measure of their generosity: "She would have been destroyed by any other place; she was permitted to 'be' only in that context, and no one stoned her or killed her or threw her out."[21]

Clearly, however, the town needs Sula as much as or perhaps more than she needs it. In giving the novel an extraordinary sense of place,[22] Morrison builds the community's character around its defense against this internal threat. Sula is not the only danger, but for a time she is the most compelling. Her defiance unifies the community by objectifying its danger. Women protected their husbands; husbands embraced their wives and children. "In general [everyone] band[ed] together against the devil in their midst" (102). No one considered destroying Sula or running her out of town. They had lived with evil and misfortune all of their lives; it "was something to be first recognized, then dealt with, survived, outwitted, triumphed over" (102).

The predominant evil in their lives, more pervasive and enduring than Sula, is the external force of oppression. Morrison's characteristic treatment of bigotry is not to delineate the defining episodes of white hatred but instead to direct attention to the black community's ingenious methods of coping: using humor, garnering strength from folk traditions, and perversely refusing to be surprised or defeated by experience. Residents of the Bottom waste little time complaining and get on with the business of their lives. Morrison captures here, as she does elsewhere, the rhythms of the black community: men on the street corner, in pool halls; women shelling peas, cooking dinner, at the beauty parlor, in church, interpreting dreams, and playing the numbers, working roots.

Yet, Morrison says, the music and dance belie the pain of men without work and of families living on the frayed edges of the prosperous white town below. Each contact with life beyond the borders of the Bottom recalls the isolating constraints of race prejudice: Helene's brutal reminder by the train conductor that her place is in the car with the other blacks; Sula and Nel's encounter with the four white teenagers who determine the physical boundaries of the girl's world by forcing them to walk in roundabout circuitous routes home from school; Shadrack's arrest by police who find him "wandering" in the white part of town. Even dead Chicken Little's space is designated by the bargeman who drays the child's body from the river, dumps it into a burlap sack, and tosses it in a corner. The sheriff's reports that "they didn't have no niggers in their country, but that some lived in those hills "cross the river, up above Medallion," (54) underscores the expectation that black life will not spill out of the hills. Morrison acknowledges the destructiveness of this enforced separation, but she also treats the isolation ironically by converting its negative meaning into a positive one. Cordoned off as they are, the people are self-sufficient; they create a neighborhood within those hills "which they could not break"[23] because it gives continuity to their past and present.

In assigning character to the Bottom, Morrison establishes worth in terms of human relationships. As she says:

> there was this life-giving very, very strong sustenance that people got from the neighborhood. . . . All the responsibilities that agencies now have were the responsibilities of the neighborhood. So that people were taken care of, or locked up or whatever. If they were sick, other people took care of them; if they were old, other people took care of them; if they needed something to eat, other people took care of them; if they were mad, other people provided a small space for them, or related to their madness or tried to find out the limits of their madness.[24]

Shadrack's presence in the Bottom is evidence of the community's willingness to absorb the most bizarre of its own. When Shadrack returns from World War I and does not know "who or what he was . . . with no past, no language, no tribe" (10), he struggles "to order and focus experience" (12) and to conquer his fear of death. The result is National Suicide Day, which Shadrack establishes as the third of January, believing "that if one day a year were devoted to it [death] everybody could get it out of the way and the rest of the year would be safe and free" (586). At first frightened of him, in time people embrace him and his day. Once they "understood the boundaries and nature of his madness, they could fit him, so to speak, into the scheme of things" (13). That is, according to Morrison, the black community's way.

Sula's mother, Hannah, and grandmother Eva had borne their share of these community responsibilities in the big house where youth, old age, disease, and insanity kept company. (Eva takes the life of her son, Plum, but Morrison treats it as an act of compassion, not of selfishness.) Sula is different, however. In refusing to become a part of the community, she refuses a part of her cultural and personal history. Her determination to define herself and to redefine a woman's role places her at odds with the community. And yet, the community makes room for her in a way perhaps that no other place would. There are both variety and cohesiveness in the Bottom, where characters as unlike as Sula, Nel, Ajax, and Shadrack coexist. "There are hundreds of small towns" like Medallion, Morrison explains, "and that's where most black people live. . . . And that's where the juices came from and that's where we *made it*, not made it in terms of success but made who we are."[25]

Morrison suggests that this quality of neighborhood life is endangered. As the buildings and trees are leveled in the Bottom to make room for a new golf course and as blacks leave the hills to occupy spaces vacated by whites in the valley below, Morrison wonders if economic and social gains are worth the sacrifice of community, because without community the cultural traditions that inform character are lost to future generations.

Notes

1. I am using the term *sequel* broadly to suggest a continuation of theme rather than a continuation of plot and identifiable characters. The novels reflect Morrison's desire to follow up her exploration of female friendships in childhood and adulthood.

2. Nellie Y. McKay, "An Interview with Toni Morrison," *Contemporary Literature* 24 (Winter 1983): 413–29. Rpt. in *Toni Morrison: Critical Perspectives Past*

and Present, ed. Henry Louis Gates, Jr., and K. A. Appiah (New York: Amistad, 1993) 399.

3. Robert B. Stepto, "'Intimate Things in Place'": A Conversation with Toni Morrison," *Massachusetts Review* 18 (Autumn 1977): 473–89. Rpt. in *Toni Morrison: Critical Perspectives Past and Present,* ed. Henry Louis Gates, Jr., and K. A. Appiah (New York: Amistad, 1993) 386.

4. Toni Morrison, *The Bluest Eye* (New York: Holt, Rinehart and Winston, 1970) 3. Subsequent references will appear in parentheses in the text.

5. Toni Morrison, "Unspeakable Things Unspoken: The Afro-American Presence in American Literature," *Michigan Quarterly Review* 28 (Winter 1989): 20.

6. Morrison, "Unspeakable" 21.
7. Morrison, "Unspeakable" 22.

8. Michael Awkward, "'The Evil of Fulfillment': Scapegoating and Narration in *The Bluest Eye,*" *Inspiriting Influences, Tradition, Revision, and Afro-American Women's Novels* (New York: Columbia University Press, 1989) 75. See also Chikwenye Ogunyemi's "Order and Disorder in Toni Morrison's *The Bluest Eye,*" *Critique: Studies in Modern Fiction* 19 (1977): 112–20.

9. Stepto 386.

10. Stepto 384.

11. Morrison, "Unspeakable" 23.

12. Morrison "Unspeakable" 23.

13. Timothy B. Powell, "Toni Morrison: The Struggle to Depict the Black Figure on the White Page," *Black American Literature Forum* 24 (Winter 1990): 752. For other clever readings of the Dick and Jane story in *The Bluest Eye,* see Shelly Wong, "Transgression as Poesis in *The Bluest Eye,*" *Callaloo* 13 (Summer 1990): 471–81; Phyllis Klotman, "Dick-and-Jane and the Shirley Temple Sensibility in *The Bluest Eye,*" *Black American Literature Forum* 13 (Winter 1979): 123–25; and others.

14. Stepto 389.

15. Stepto 388.

16. Toni Morrison, *Sula,* (New York: Alfred A. Knopf, 1973) 44. Subsequent references will appear in parentheses in the text.

17. Maureen T. Reddy ("The Tripled Plot and Center of *Sula,*" *Black American Literature Forum* 22 (Spring 1988) 29–45) enlarges this view of Sula's deficiencies. Reddy, surprisingly, labels Sula a woman with "no true inner core of self [who] tries to appropriate Nel's by doing what Nel does, including having sex with Jude" (37). According to Reddy, "In spite of her deathbed claim that she 'sure did live in this world' and her insistence that she owns herself, Sula never reaches real self understanding because she has no abiding self to understand nor any way of creating a self . . ." (37). Reddy's interpretation does not negate the view that Sula inspires Nel to act imaginatively. What Sula does not have and what Nel offers her is definition and order. Each has something that the other needs.

18. Stepto 381.

19. Stepto 382.

20. Claudia Tate, "Conversation with Toni Morrison," *Black Women Writers at Work,* ed. Claudia Tate (New York: Continuum Publishing Co., 1983) 125–26.

21. Tate 343.

22. All of Morrison's novels have an extraordinary sense of place, but in *Sula* the author says she felt place "very strongly, not in terms of the country or the state, but in terms of the details, the feeling, the mood of the community, of the town." See Stepto 378.

23. Stepto 379.

24. Stepto 379.

25. Stepto 380.

3

Male Consciousness
Song of Solomon

When asked during an interview if she thinks her novels are evolutionary, Morrison responded that she believes they are: "from a book that focused on a pair of very young black girls . . . to a pair of adult black women, and then to a black man . . . is evolutionary."[1] The black man Morrison speaks about is the subject of her third novel, *Song of Solomon* (1977). (*Song of Solomon* greatly enhanced Morrison's literary reputation and broadened her reading audience. It was a Book-of-the-Month Club selection—the first, it has been widely noted, by a black writer since Richard Wright's *Native Son* in 1940—and a year after its publication 570,000 copies were in print.) Ajax and Cholly, the men who took shape in previous novels, were drawn in outline and may be viewed as previews of the more-detailed male characters in *Song of Solomon* and in later novels. In *Song of Solomon*, Morrison scrutinizes friendship, marriage, family, and relationship to community, primarily (but not exclusively) from men's points of view. Such scrutiny is driven by Morrison's belief that a man's experience of life is different from a woman's. Maleness "tends to be inherent," she believes, in spite of "eighty per cent of the literature" to the contrary.[2] Morrison realizes that her comments may be "astonishing" to some and that male and female roles may be learned, but she still holds to an idea of masculinity. Based on her observations of two brothers, a father, and sons, she concludes that men have "different spatial requirements than girls," they relate "to architecture and space differently"; her sons "were attracted to danger and risk" in a way she was not, and on the "question of dominion" men, she says, have "a definite need to exercise dominion over place and people." They "desire to control" in a way that women do not.[3]

Milkman Dead's major conflict of values in the novel exemplifies, to some extent, gender-determined perspectives: as a son he feels immense pressure to embrace his father's affection for things. But Morrison, as an artist concerned with dimensions of spirituality, offers Milkman an alternative to the pursuit of material success: spiritual fulfillment. Milkman, as one would expect, chooses spirituality, and in explicating his judgment, Morrison retraces her precise boundaries of freedom and responsibility for the individual. Like other Morrison characters who would be spiritually free, Milkman must be willing to resist all narrow definitions of the self and take responsibility for the tough choices he makes.

Macon Dead, Milkman's father, has lost this essential freedom; he has traded it for wealth under the mistaken belief that "money is freedom. . . . The only real freedom there is."[4] Macon advises his son to "own things. And let the things you own own other things. Then you'll own yourself and other people too" (55). But despite his thinking so, property does not elevate Macon above other blacks or earn him respect from whites. In truth, blacks do not hold him in high esteem; they merely fear his ruthless exercise of power, and corrupt whites respect not him but his money. A lifetime of acquiring property, collecting rents, and making deals has rendered Macon a greedy, self-absorbed, unforgiving (and unforgiven) man who is incapable of showing love or of receiving it. Hating his wife, Ruth, ignoring his daughters, Lena and First Corinthians, and disowning his sister, Pilate, are the sum of Macon's family connections. Even the one relationship—with Milkman—which promises to humanize him is contaminated by their scheme to steal the gold that he thinks his sister possesses. Family for Macon is just another category of personal wealth. His Sunday drives in the new Packard with Ruth and Milkman in the front seat and Corinthians and Lena in the back are merely parades of possessions. The lifeless metallic form of the Packard, which the people in the community dub "Macon Dead's hearse," is a looming symbol of the dead relationships and feelings of the people inside.

At age thirty-two Milkman is his father's son. The macho rebellion of adolescence has been replaced by a self-indulgent callousness and a tacit acceptance of his father's way. Collecting Macon's rents, partying with bourgeois blacks who spend silly hours imitating the leisure of whites— these anchor Milkman's life, "which was pointless, aimless, and it was true that he didn't concern himself an awful lot about other people. There was nothing he wanted bad enough to risk anything for, inconvenience himself for" (107). As it is with his father, family for Milkman is a burdensome afterthought. His interactions with them—all women—is mostly an exercise in male prerogative. In fact, he had never really "been able to distinguish them [his sisters] from his mother" (68). Once he had knocked his father into a wall for hitting his mother, but that was less a display of regard for his mother's welfare than a startling instance of arrogance. The younger man had bested the older and, in doing so, felt a "snorting, horse-galloping glee as old as desire" (68). Coming to his mother's defense is a singular instance for Milkman. More typical of his filial tie to her is the unresponsiveness revealed in a "dream" that he relates to his friend Guitar. In Milkman's vision Ruth is in the backyard garden planting tulip bulbs which immediately sprout "bloody red heads" that grow tall and menacing. Eventually, as Milkman watches from the kitchen window, the smothering plants suffocate his mother, who "was kicking to the last" (105). When Guitar asks, "Why didn't you go help her?" Milkman's uncomprehending retort is "what?" Attending to others has never seemed necessary or beneficial to Milkman. As his sister Lena observes, Milkman's has been a thoughtless life of self-gratification: "You have yet to wash your underwear, spread a bed, wipe the ring from your tub, or move a fleck of your dirt from one place to another. And to this day, you have never asked one of us if we were tired, or sad, or wanted a cup of coffee. . . . You are a sad, pitiful, stupid, selfish, hateful man. I hope your little hog's gut stands you in good stead, and that you take good care of it, because you don't have anything else" (217–18). Lena's accusations shock Milkman into a necessary but unfortunately shallow self-examination, and the conclusions he reaches illustrate his profound shortsightedness: he will find the gold his father thinks Pilate stole from a cave in Pennsylvania and declare his independence. With enough money he would be free of all human obligations. Such thinking reveals Milkman's incredible conceit. His soul, like his mirror image, lacks "coherence, a coming together of the features into a total" (70).

In many ways Milkman's journey from his home in Michigan to Pennsylvania to Kentucky and back home conforms to the classical male monomyth of the heroic quest. In this structure the hero's adventure takes him on a journey beset with mortal danger but a journey which, in the end, brings him nobility and great honor among his people. Of course, Morrison does not faithfully, nor with a straight face, appropriate the monomyth paradigm to her story and character. She admits that *Song of Solomon* is her "own giggle (in Afro-American terms) of the proto-myth of the journey to manhood."[5] She feels that "whenever characters are cloaked in Western fable, they are in deep trouble."[6] One kind of trouble is the customary designation of male narrative as more imperative than female narrative. Morrison would, no doubt, decline to identify her novel with a narrative tradition so antithetical to her aesthetic, which makes her consistently attentive to women's narratives even in a text like *Song of Solomon*, which is primarily devoted to men's experiences. Instead, then, of blithely conceiving Milkman's journey in terms of the traditional hero's, Morrison satirically calls attention to limitations of the traditional quest by making Milkman less heroic and more human.[7] Not a classical hero, Milkman is a contemporary black man lost to his community, family, and, most important, lost to himself. His true quest is not for fortune or honor but for his humanity.

Every phase of his search for gold brings Milkman closer to these truths. In Danville, Pennsylvania, Fred Garnett, a passing motorist, teaches Milkman that not everyone is motivated by financial gain. When Milkman offers him money to pay for a Coke and a ride from the country into town, Garnett shakes his head in disgust and disbelief. Milkman learns that one man can give another "a Coke and a lift now and then" (257) without expecting payment. Reverend Cooper's stories about "old Macon Dead," Milkman's grandfather, about Lincoln's Heaven, the farm that he worked and loved, about the old man's son, Macon Dead, Jr., who worked "right alongside" his father, reveal for the first time to Milkman the powerful balm in the phrase "I know your people!" (231). As he listens to the old men's recollections of the past, "He glittered in the light of their adoration and grew fierce with pride" (238). These experiences in Danville begin to unravel Milkman's webbing of indifference just as the difficult country terrain where he searches for the gold spoils the superficial finery of his clothes. By the time he returns to town, Milkman has experienced, in the river stream where he loses his balance and falls in, the first baptismal to a new life. His three-piece suit and Florsheim shoes are soiled and torn, his "heavy over-designed" (240) watch is splintered, the minute hand broken as if to signal an eruption. In the country he comes face to face with his limitations. "He had no idea that simply walking through trees, bushes, on untrammeled ground could be so hard. Woods always brought to his mind city parks, the tended woods on Honore Island where he went for outings as a child and where tiny convenient paths led you through" (252). But here Milkman is alone, far from a town, in a place where his father's money is irrelevant. Here he must chart his own course. And that course must be one that takes him away from old paths of indolence, greed, and vanity toward new paths of spiritual enlightenment. Milkman still has far to travel. The journey so far has brought him to an appreciation of family and hard work that he did not have before, but buried treasure continues to make a slave of him. He does not yet know that money cannot buy the kind of freedom he needs.

This insight is not available to Milkman until the second phase of his journey in Shalimar, Virginia. Pilate may have gone there, he thinks, and buried the gold. In this small southern community with no commerce or industry, what is left of Milkman's flashy affluence is insolent to the people who live there: his casual willingness simply to buy a car to replace the broken one he bought the day before, the insult of locking his car against the men he has asked for help, calling them "them," not bothering to give his name or ask theirs. "He was telling them that they weren't men . . . that thin shoes and suits with vests . . . were the measure" (269). The possum hunt, however, that Milkman is goaded into joining changes all of that. Finally, stripped of everything except his watch (and he will soon lose that), dressed in brogans, army fatigues, and a knit cap, Milkman, like the other hunters, must take his measure against the laws of nature. Survival depends upon penetrating the darkness, traversing the rocky terrain, interpreting the dogs' barks, anticipating his prey, sending wordless messages to his companions.

Milkman is not up to this work, and he is nearly conquered by fatigue and fear. But with these trials come flashes of genuine insight (not the shallow self-examination of a few weeks earlier). He now realizes that the black men of Shalimar are more than the sum of money they might earn in city factories or from rent collections. Their primordial link to the earth, to animals, and to each other inspires Milkman's respect. For "if they could talk to animals, and the animals could talk to them, what didn't they know about human beings? Or the earth itself, for that matter" (280). Since he can do none of these, Milkman must acknowledge his own glaring limitations in this place:

> There was nothing here to help him—not his money, his car, his father's reputation, his suit, or his shoes. In fact they hampered him. Except for his broken watch, and his wallet with about two hundred dollars, all he had started out with on his journey was gone: his suitcase with the scotch, the shirts, and the space for bags of gold; his snap-brim hat, his tie, his shirt, his three-piece suit, his socks, and his shoes. His watch and his two hundred dollars would be of no help out here, where all a man had was what he was born with, or had learned to use. And endurance. Eyes, ears, nose, taste, touch—and some other sense that he knew he did not have. (280)

Milkman's reveries have a domino effect, toppling one illusion after another: money is not freedom, but enslavement; independence means submitting himself to people in his life, not escaping them. He confesses and repents of his shameful retreat from relationships—refusing any involvement in his parent's problems, using Hagar's love and then throwing it "away like a wad of chewing gum after the flavor was gone" (280), betraying Pilate, the one who had saved his life and then loved him unconditionally. Alone, without the accoutrement of his vanity, the old personality gives way to make space for a new spirituality so expansive that only "the whole entire complete deep blue sea!" (330) will contain its volume.

In Shalimar, after the hunt, a transformed Milkman engages a woman's generosity with his—for the first time in his life and without hesitation. Sweet, "a nice lady up the road a ways" (288), takes Milkman in, bathes his sore body, and tends his hurts. In return Milkman gives her a cool bath, rubbing and soaping her "until her skin squeaked and glistened like onyx" (288). He washes her hair, massages her back, makes her bed, washes her dishes, and scours her tub. His unselfish attentions to Sweet are a striking contrast to his inattention to the other women in his life, especially his cousin, Hagar, and a lock of Hagar's hair in his wallet will be a persistent reminder that she died forlorn, with the sound of his spiteful words resonating in his wake. When he was a little boy making the obligatory Sunday drives with his father, mother, and sisters, Milkman had disliked kneeling on the front seat and looking out the back windows in order to see anything. "Riding backwards made him uneasy. It was like flying blind and not knowing where he was going—just where he had been" (31–32). Yet, now he must do just that. In order to move forward with his life, he must review where he has been.

That is the heroic journey for Morrison's characters: to press towards knowledge for its own sake. Morrison holds Milkman responsible for his transgressions, but she also forgives him. "He was not in a position to do anything about [them] . . . because he was stupid," she says. In the future he can "do better, and don't do *that* again."[8] It is important to Morrison that her characters "have revelations, large or small."[9]

The new Milkman is a striking contrast to the other male characters in the novel, who are not transcendent. Macon Dead and Guitar Bains are shaped by ugly circumstances over which they have no control. Each (over)reacts to his helplessness with a compulsive and unremarkable will to conquer. Macon's greedy obsession with owning things and people is a mutated version of his love, as a child, of the land and his family. Belonging to the earth, working with his father, caring for his sister, and earning respect and admiration from the black community define Macon's child-hood. His father's violent death at the hands of powerful white men who take the land change love to obsession. "Owning, building, acquiring—that was his life, his future, his present, and all the history he knew. That he distorted life, bent it, for the sake of gain, was a measure of his loss at his father's death" (304). Proprietorship consumes Macon and alienates him from family and community, leaving no room for spiritual virtues like love, compassion, kindness, tolerance. He loves only the keys to buildings that he carries in his pocket and that he fondles often and reassuringly. Morrison offers them as a symbol of his empty victory.

Similarly, when Guitar's anger over white brutality against blacks impels him to join the Seven Days as their Sunday man, the anger inside implodes, and he becomes what he hates—a murderer. Like Macon, Guitar is a victim of his experience. Although he is a self-declared avenger of his people, the love of black life is eventually twisted into a love of power. That power gives him, he thinks, authority which he uses to kill indiscriminately—white and black.

Guitar and Milkman are opposite sides of a single fabric, and Morrison constructs their friendship from the threads of male life—street fights, bar-bershop talk, pool hall banter, sexual conquest, adventure—just as she constructs Nel and Sula's friendship from the threads of women's lives. Guitar's wild courage excites the sheltered Milkman. Guitar is older than Milkman and street-smart. He protects Milkman, he initiates him to street life, and he does not blame the son for the sins of his father. As Guitar reminds a friend who refuses to serve beer to the underaged Milkman for fear of Macon's retaliation, "You can't blame him for who his daddy is."

As the easy laughter of their adolescent intimacy gives way to conflict that throws their differences into stark relief, Morrison uses the space to examine black militancy, not in the service of advocacy, but as a way of characterizing the spectrum of black response to white violence in the 1960s. Some, like Milkman, convinced themselves that white oppression of blacks did not concern them. Others, like Macon Dead, turned white hatred into self-hatred and in turn directed that hatred toward their own people. Dia-metrically, Guitar and the Seven Days, enraged by the lynchings, the burnings, the murder, respond in kind. For them white hatred precipitates acts of black love. "What I'm doing ain't about hating white people," Gui-tar tells his friend, "It's about loving us. About loving you. My whole life is love" (160). In pledging his "whole life" to the universal love of all black people, Guitar cannot claim a more personal love of wife, children, friends.

The secrecy of his work isolates him and precludes intimacy. Eventually, the appealing interplay of street wisdom and hard-edged generosity that defines Guitar gives way to brooding paranoia.

The complementing differences in Guitar's and Milkman's personalities that make each part of a whole are not the differences that eventually divide them. They become competing personalities, unrecognizable to each other. As Milkman journeys toward self-discovery and cultural identification, Guitar travels a parallel road toward psychic disintegration and cultural alienation. The belonging and understanding that Milkman recovers on the hunt in Shalimar are lost to Guitar, who once shared the camaraderie of the hunt as a child. But now in the woods he feels not brotherhood but murderous hostility. He is diseased with "white madness"—the bizarre executions of total strangers. Black crimes are not freakish in that way, according to Morrison. Blacks commit crimes "in the heat of passion: anger, jealousy, loss of face, and so on" (109). (Even the Seven Days, though their crimes are deliberate and premeditated, fall within some broad boundary of legitimacy since their work is a response to aggression.) But stalking Milkman and killing Pilate, whose healing, ancestral guidance he rejects in favor of street justice, place Guitar outside all boundaries of rationality and morality. There can be no moral authority in killing for gold or for pleasure.

In a role reversal, as their journeys come to an end, it is Milkman who draws closest to achieving genuine universal love. His final leap from the rock is not the theatrical miscalculation of a disillusioned man wearing blue silk wings that opens *Song of Solomon* but a hard-earned conviction that, like Pilate, he has courage enough to face any episode of life—even death. When Milkman first gleans these truths, he longs to share them with Guitar, but he can only mourn Guitar's loss. Like Nel and Sula's, Milkman and Guitar's breakup is irreparable.

To his credit Milkman empathizes with his friend and with his father and is able to forgive their transgressions. Indications are that he even forgives Pilate's murder. "You want my life?" Milkman calls out to Guitar in the aftermath of the shooting. "You want it? Here" (341). Milkman's tearful offer of himself, even in the service of Guitar's corrupt need, would seem to suggest that Milkman has evolved to the point that he values love more than he values the physical world. Many readers decry what they believe is the deliberate ambiguity of Morrison's conclusion, which does not explore Guitar's guilt and/or remorse and does not resolve Milkman's feelings: does he leap toward Guitar in anger or in love? But understanding what may appear ambiguous requires remembering Morrison's commitment to readers' participation in making meaning by leaving "spaces" in the text. She explains that "into these spaces should fall the rumination of the reader and his or her invented or recollected or misunderstood knowingness."[10] Each reader interprets text in terms that reflect her experiences. Even with that stipulation to readers, however, Morrison does explain that in the final scenes Guitar recognizes Milkman's transformation "and recalls enough of how lost he himself is . . . to put his weapon down"[11] and perhaps rises up to meet Milkman's gesture of love with a comparable one. Ultimately, however, there is always something more "interesting at stake than a clear resolution in a novel"[12] for Morrison. She is more occupied with her character's survival and with the "complexity of how people behave under duress— . . . the qualities they show at the end of an event when their backs are up against the wall."[13] Milkman's response under duress is to accept what Pilate already knew—that there is no reason to fear death if the spirit is freed in life.

Milkman's unfettered spirit is marked by a dream about flying, Morrison's metaphor for the unconventional life of spiritual freedom. In Sweet's bed he dreams "about sailing high over the earth. . . . Part of his flight was over the dark sea, but it didn't frighten him because he knew he could not fall" (302). As a child Milkman had longed for physical flight, and his discovery at age four that "only birds and airplanes could fly" had made him lose "all interest in himself" (9). The result is a dull, unimaginative childhood that stretches into a pointless, indifferent adulthood. Flying remains a literal conception, impossible to achieve except on his first airplane ride, where "in the air, away from real life, he felt free" (222). Freedom in an airplane "away from real life" is illusory, however. Milkman does not yet know that it is the spirit which must soar. As the insurance agent Robert Smith discovers, in modern times, believing in literal flight is a mental aberration that leads to certain death on the street below. In Michigan, Milkman is wedded to the streets where he estimates his worth in the marketplace in terms of money and commodities. Milkman is like the peacock he chases at the car lot, moored by the weight of his own finery. Guitar could just as easily be describing Milkman when he observes that the peacock has "too much tail. All that jewelry weighs it down. Like vanity. Can't nobody fly with all that shit. Wanna fly. You got to give up the shit that weighs you down" (179–80). In Virginia, Milkman "gives up" the vanity acquired on Not Doctor Street when he accepts the timeless rhythms of men and animals in the woods.

Flight, the free fall, consistently means freedom, independence, un-conventionality, self-knowledge for Morrison. In *Song of Solomon* flight also evokes the American folk tradition.[14] Solomon's song is Morrison's version of the flying African myth about enslaved Africans who escaped slavery in the South by rising up and flying back to Africa and to freedom. In adopting and adapting the myth, Morrison becomes the modern griot, reciting stories from the past to a new generation. And her novel serves an essential function as cultural artifact. Myths are forgotten or misunder-stood, Morrison thinks, because people in transit move away from the places where they were born and from the culture bearers who remain in those places. The flying myth is her example of one that is misunderstood by those who can relate to it in Western classical terms only. But Morrison wishes to restore its tutorial power for black people. As she says:

> If it means Icarus to some readers, fine; I want to take credit for that. But my meaning is specific: it is about black people who could fly. That was always part of the folklore of my life; flying was one of our gifts. I don't care how silly it may seem. It is everywhere—people used to talk about it, it's in the spirituals and gospels. Perhaps it was wishful thinking—escape, death, and all that. But suppose it wasn't. What might it mean? I tried to find out in *Song of Solomon.*[15]

When Milkman realizes that the children's song "Solomon done fly, Solomon done gone / Solomon cut across the sky, Solomon gone home" is about his great-great-grandfather Solomon, who had such powers, he rejoices: Solomon "didn't need no airplane. He just took off; got fed up. All the way up! No more cotton! No more bales! No more orders! No more shit! He flew, baby. Lifted his beautiful black ass up in the sky and flew on home" (332). Milkman is exhilarated, but Morrison is cautious. African myth is not less vulnerable to contamination than Western fable. Solomon flew off, and Morrison asks, "Who'd he leave behind?" (332). What about the wife and twenty-one children that he left here on the ground?

With that question Morrison's novel about male consciousness signals her ongoing delineation of women's concerns. Solomon flies off, and Ryna, his wife, is left to take care of the children. Her cries of protest and anguish are still carried on the wind more than a century later for Milkman to hear. In the third generation Milkman and Hagar reenact this tragedy of aban-donment. When Milkman leaves, Hagar loses all capacity to think ratio-nally, and she dies, as the euphemism goes, of a broken heart. Milkman dreams of flying as Hagar is dying (336). As always, however, Morrison intimates that matters of freedom and responsibility are not so easily settled. Milkman is, without a doubt, culpable. He has been callous and careless. But does Hagar's love for him give her the right to demand his love in return? Morrison answers no. Guitar reminds Hagar that "love shouldn't be like that" (309). Love is not possession. "You can't own a human being" (310). And most important you cannot love someone more than you love yourself. Hagar, who "wanted to kill for love, die for love," (310) has not learned these lessons. Guitar calls her one of those "doormat women" whose "pride and conceit" amazes him (310). Hagar will not or cannot save her own life because she does not value herself outside the narrow limits of Milkman's love. Her frantic efforts to make herself over to fit the popular image of female beauty continues Morrison's recurring invective against the tyranny of such an image. Morrison's description of the carnival of smells, colors, and textures at the cosmetics counter in the department store where Hagar goes is a tour de force of the seductive influences of commercial marketing stratagems:

> The cosmetics department enfolded her in perfume, and she read hungrily the labels and the promise. Myrurgia for primeval woman who created for him a world of tender privacy where the only occupant is you, mixed with Nina Ricci's L'Air du Temps. Yardley's Flair with Tuvache's Nectaroma and D'Orsay's Intoxication. Robert Piquet's Fracas, and Calypso and Visa and Bandit. Houbigant's Chantilly. Caron's Fleurs de Rocaille and Bellodgia. Hagar breathed deeply the sweet air that hung over the glass counters. Like a smiling sleepwalker she circled. Round and round the diamond-clear counters covered with bottled, wafer-thin disks, round boxes, tubes, and phials. Lipsticks in soft white hands darted out of their sheaths like the shiny red penises of puppies. Peachy powders and milky lotions were grouped in front of poster after cardboard poster of gorgeous grinning faces. Faces in ecstasy. Faces somber with achieved seduction. Hagar believed she could spend her life there among the cut glass, shimmering in peaches and cream, in satin. In opulence. In luxe. In love. (315)

Hagar is bound for disappointment as the promises of cosmetic beauty are washed away with the scents and powders in a pouring rain on the street outside the department store. Morrison's work is a warning shot for those who would be victim to a false standard of beauty like Hagar and like Pauline Breedlove before her. Morrison's heroic characters must resist; they must be transformed, not cosmetically, but internally by their own humanity, and like Milkman they must take responsibility for their own lives.

Milkman's journey shapes his metamorphosis so that by the novel's conclusion he has achieved freedom and accountability. Intuitive, compassionate, forgiving, generous, he knows that "if you surrendered to the air, you could *ride* it" (341).

Pilate is the other heroic character in *Song of Solomon*. Her journey to self-knowledge having been completed, she knows, from the beginning of the text, what Milkman discovers in the end, and as her name suggests, Pilate is Milkman's spiritual guide throughout his passage. During Milkman's infancy and even before, she shields him from Macon's angry attacks, and later, during Milkman's adolescence, she catalyzes his course of self-discovery. In her presence, at age twelve, he discovers a woman, who without property and social position, is taller and wiser than his father. That "was the first time in his life that [he] remembered being completely happy" (47). Pilate's stories about her life on the farm, about her father's bravery, about her brother's love, and her refusal to adopt the meaningless rituals that occupy most people—these counter Macon's stories about conquest, ownership, and dominion. Macon's declaration to his son that "Pilate can't teach you a thing you can use in the world" (55) proves false, for Pilate alone teaches him the true meaning of flying without ever leaving the ground (340). Pilate's is not the selfish flight of Solomon, who leaves everyone behind. Pilate teaches Milkman that "you can't fly on off and leave a body" (336). When Milkman leaves Hagar, it is Pilate who locks him in her cellar upon his return, forcing his dawning realization that Hagar is dead, that "it was his fault and Pilate knew it" (336). His punishment by Pilate's reckoning is to carry with him "something that remained of the life he had taken" (336). That evening Milkman returns home with a box of Hagar's hair as a healing reminder that with freedom comes responsibility.

Pilate, of course, is one of Morrison's ancestors, one of the timeless people who dispatch their wisdom to others, who consciously or unconsciously initiate others to the ways of African-American culture that give life continuity and intent. Out of place in "the big northern city" (266) Pilate embraces more natural rhythms like those of the women of Shalimar who walk the road without purses, "bare-legged, their unstraightened hair braided or pulled straight back into a ball" (266). Pilate has little need for the creature comforts of "elaborately socialized society" (150). In deciding early in her life whom she wanted to love and what was important to her, Pilate has given up interest in manners and money but has "acquired a deep concern for and about human relationships" (150).

Ancestral, mythic, free, Pilate embodies memorable traits of character that give form to the major theme of Morrison's work: spiritual transcendence. Born without a navel, which evidences the common birth of one human from another, Pilate seems ageless, immortal. As a natural healer whose "compassion for troubled people" and "respect for other people's privacy" (150) are her passport, she has no fear of life. Neither does she have the familiar terror of death: "she spoke often to the dead [and] . . . knew there was nothing to fear" (149). At the end of her life, Milkman wonders if there is another like Pilate. "There's got to be at least one more woman like you," he whispers (340). As ancestor Pilate bears a major share of the novel's work in passing on cultural knowledge to Milkman and to the reader.

All of Morrison's novels mirror the characters, language, folklore, mythology of African America. In *Song of Solomon*, Morrison nudges cultural memory by examining the importance in the black community of names and naming. Names of places and people are routinely appended, denoting some exploit or episode or special skill or talent or notoriety. Names have meaning; names tell stories: Ryna's Gulch, Solomon's Leap, Not Doctor Street—once called Doctor Street (its official name is Mains Avenue) by blacks in honor of the first black man to practice medicine in the city who lived and died on Doctor Street. When the white city legislators posted notices in businesses on the street reminding residents of the avenue's official name, Southside residents deliberately and unceremoniously took up Not Doctor Street, a name which signaled their inventive resistance to any oppression. Milkman (whose name is one old man's idea of humor) considers the import of black men and women knowing their names:

> Names they got from yearnings, gestures, flaws, events, mistakes, weaknesses. Names that bore witness. Macon Dead, Sing Byrd, Crowell Byrd, Pilate, Reba, Hagar, Magdalene, First Corinthians, Milkman, Guitar, Railroad Tommy, Hospital Tommy, Empire State (he just stood around and swayed), Small Boy, Sweet, Circe, Moon, Nero, Humpty-Dumpty, Blue Boy, Scandinavia, Quack-Quack, Jericho, Spoonbread, Ice Man, Dough Belly, Rocky River, Gray Eye, Cock-a-Doodle Doo, Cool Breeze, Muddy Waters, Pinetop, Jelly Roll, Fats, Lead-Belly, Bo Diddley, Cat-Iron, Peg-Leg, Son, Shortstuff, Smoky Babe, Funny Papa, Bukka, Pink, Bull Moose, B.B., T-Bone, Black Ace, Lemon, Washboard, Gatemouth, Cleanhead, Tampa Red, Juke Boy, Shine, Staggerlee, Jim the Devil, Fuck-up, and *Dat* Nigger. (333–34)

To know one's name is to own it, to insist upon claiming its history. Milkman learns to accept his name as a testimony to the loneliness that kept his mother nursing him until he was old enough to dangle his legs to the floor. Jake keeps and owns the unfortunate name given him by an illiterate white man and passes that name on to his son, who passes it on to his son. Pilate keeps "her own name and everybody else's," Guitar thinks (89), in a brass box attached to her ear. Perhaps she understands as Milkman does that "when you know your name you should hang on to it, for unless it is noted down and remembered, it will die when you do" (333). As Morrison explains it, the gold of Milkman's search "is really Pilate's yellow orange and the glittering metal of the box in her ear" (29) containing her name. In the opening epigraph of *Song of Solomon*, Morrison reminds that "the fathers may soar / And the children may know their names." Each generation is obliged to remember and pass its knowledge on to the next.

Notes

1. Nellie Y. McKay, "An Interview with Toni Morrison," *Contemporary Literature* 24 (Winter 1983): 413–29. Rpt. in *Toni Morrison: Critical Perspectives Past and Present,* ed. Henry Louis Gates, Jr., and K. A. Appiah (New York: Amistad, 1993) 399.

2. Rosemarie K. Lester, "An Interview with Toni Morrison, Hessian Radio Network, Frankfurt, West Germany," *Critical Essays on Toni Morrison,* ed. Nellie Y. McKay (Boston: G. K. Hall & Co., 1988) 48.

3. Lester 47–48.

4. Toni Morrison, *Song of Solomon* (New York: Alfred A. Knopf, 1977) 163. Subsequent references will appear in parentheses in the text.

5. Toni Morrison, "Unspeakable Things Unspoken: The Afro-American Presence in American Literature," *Michigan Quarterly Review* 28 (Winter 1989) 29.

6. Morrison, "Unspeakable" 29.

7. For a discussion of Morrison's inversion of the male monomyth, see Gerry Brenner, *"Song of Solomon:* Morrison's Rejection of Rank's Monomyth and Feminism," *Studies in American Fiction* 15 (Spring 1987): 13–24. For a discussion of Morrison's use of female narrative to counteract male narrative, see Michael Awkward, "'Unruly and Let Loose': Myth, Ideology, and Gender in *Song of Solomon,*" *Callaloo* 13 (Summer 1990): 482–98.

8. McKay 403.

9. McKay 406.

10. Morrison, "Unspeakable" 29.

11. Morrison, "Unspeakable" 29.

12. McKay 402.

13. McKay 402.

14. Although Morrison finds the comparison unflattering, some see parallels between Milkman's quest and the quests in the works of William Faulkner and between images of flying in *Song of Solomon* and James Joyce's *A Portrait of the Artist as a Young Man*. David Cowart discusses these similarities in "Faulkner and Joyce in Morrison's *Song of Solomon*," *American Literature* 62 (March 1990): 87–100.

15. Thomas LeClair, "'The Language Must Not Sweat': A Conversation with Toni Morrison," *New Republic* 184 (21 March 1981): 26–27.

4

COMMUNITY
AND CULTURAL IDENTITY
TAR BABY

Song of Solomon, due in part to its popular appeal, gave dramatic momentum to Morrison's writing career. By 1981, the year of her fourth book, *Tar Baby,* that career was soaring. As one reviewer observed, "The promotion of *Tar Baby* was a stunning show," choreographed by "the Madison Avenue machinery [which] spun into highest gear." Morrison was, the reviewer continued, "the toast of the literary world,"[1] appearing at parties and on television, giving readings, and (arguably the most remarkable of these unveilings) appearing on the 30 March 1981 cover of *Newsweek.* Morrison's by now familiar and unsentimental response to the magazine's coverage was "I can't believe *Newsweek* will have a middle-aged colored woman on its cover."

In *Tar Baby,* Morrison continues to expand the range of her subjects and characters. For the first time in her work she gives white characters significant roles. Here, they figure prominently in her examination of the intricacies of inter- and intraracial relationships. Valerian Street, a wealthy candy manufacturer, and his wife, Margaret, both come under scrutiny as employers, as husband and wife, as parents, and both perform poorly in every category. Morrison finds much to condemn and little to redeem either. And yet, she does not withhold the hope of redemption. With Morrison few crimes are beyond human understanding, and few of her characters are unworthy of her compassion. She wants readers to see not just a character's "facade" but the "point of view inside."[2] *Tar Baby* is not a protest novel; Morrison is not looking for someone to blame for white oppression of blacks. Certainly Valerian and Margaret are reflections of their social, economic, and racial backgrounds (and Morrison explores these), but she renders them more interesting as individuals, each with his or her own crimes quite apart from the rest of their race.

Valerian's complications of character demonstrate well Morrison's unwillingness to take the easy path of stereotype. Valerian is indulgently world-weary. His cynical, unromanticized view of his own orphaned youth as a candy heir surrounded by doting uncles and maiden aunts is easily applicable to his view of all social relations. Wife Margaret is tolerated as an incapable middle-aged beauty twenty years his junior. Son Michael is an irrelevant thirty-year-old social activist always in search of the next cause. And after thirty years as butler and cook, all that can be said of Sidney and Ondine is that they are at least as familiar to him as his wife and son.

It is partly this cynicism that prompts Valerian to leave Philadelphia for L'Arbe de la Croix, his residence on a remote Caribbean island, to live as a quasi hermit tending hothouse plants. On the island, unlike in the city, Valerian is shielded from people and places that have become increasingly unfamiliar. On the island he can avoid a public review of his imminent dotage. The ordered greenhouse is proof of these effects. Valerian spends days tending the plants and playing the music of European classical composers, oblivious to the natural rhythms of the island that play outside. The measured growth of the greenhouse plants is a symbol of his control. But such order amid wildness is unnatural just as Valerian's presence on Isle des Chevaliers is unnatural. Morrison personifies all of nature in protest of Valerian's intrusion. When the rain forests are destroyed to make space for opulent winter playhouses like Valerian's, "clouds of fish were convinced that the world was over" and "wild parrots . . . agreed."[3] The river, too, understood that the balance was destroyed, that "never again would the rain be equal," (7) and the two-thousand-year-old forest that had been "scheduled for eternity" was instead bound for extinction. When Valerian's dotage finally arrives, he can no longer keep the life of the island in check. Ants eat their way through the copper wires of his stereo and promise to invade the greenhouse itself, and trees are poised outside to overrun the house. "Things grew or died where and how they pleased. Isle des Chevaliers filled in the spaces that had been the island's to begin with" (208). Indeed, Morrison envisions nature's revenge: "After thirty years of shame," the champion daisy trees which had remained serene during man's assault "were marshalling for war" (236).

Beyond cynicism, Valerian suffers from the arrogance afflicting the majority of his social and economic class: the arrogance that makes rearranging the wild, beautiful island landscape to install his foreign presence possible; the arrogance that allows him "to dismiss with a flutter of the fingers the people [of the Caribbean] whose sugar and cocoa had allowed him to grow old in regal comfort" (174).

Valerian, however, does not sink completely beneath the white man's burden of responsibility for the planet's sorrow. He is in part borne up by his acts of decency: giving stocks to Sidney and Ondine; paying for their niece, Jadine's, education; paying social security taxes to prevent them from ending up like many domestic workers who spend their lives tending other people's children and kitchens with no retirement income to sustain them in old age.

Valerian is not malevolent, nor is he an ordinary bigot. To accuse him of these failings would be a sure way for Morrison to develop theme, but such a reductive characterization would not represent Valerian's "point of view inside." In Morrison's estimation Valerian is more complex and more interesting: he is innocent. For all his worldly cynicism, Valerian is essentially unaware of the harm that he has caused and that he has allowed others to cause. He does not know that his presence in the Caribbean is an extension of Western colonialism or that firing Gideon and Therese for stealing apples is immoral since he had stolen much more from them: a place in the continuing history of their island. And worst of all, he does not know that his wife is a child abuser, that Margaret systematically burned, pricked, cut their son, Michael, throughout his childhood. Valerian does not know these things "because he had not taken the trouble to know. . . . He was guilty, therefore, of innocence" (209). When it is too late to make a difference, Valerian wonders if there is anything "so loathsome as a willfully innocent man?" He realizes that "an innocent man is a sin before God." Sin is human; innocence is "inhuman and therefore unworthy. No man should live without absorbing the sins of his kind" (209). This realization pushes Valerian into sudden old age, and he must finally admit the arrogance and cynicism which have defended him against knowing. As Terry Otten demonstrates, in Morrison's fiction "those who sin against the flawed order become the agents of experience and so run the risk of freedom. Those who do not are often doomed to spiritual stasis and moral entropy."[4] In the end only those with knowledge survive.

That includes Margaret, whose point of view inside renders her larger than her crime. Her offense—horrible though it is—links her to the rest of humanity. In comparing himself to her, Valerian muses that "Margaret knew the bottomlessness—she had looked at it, dived in it and pulled herself out—obviously tougher than he" (209). Suffering all those years with the secret of what she has done earns Margaret the right to judge herself and Valerian. She can also forgive herself and ultimately feels tranquillity and contentment. Morrison comes close to empathizing with Margaret as a woman like other women victimized by a society that overvalues physical beauty. Born beautiful into a family of plain parents and ordinary siblings, Margaret is ignored, despised, and finally left alone to make what she will of her assets. She is the teenage object of Valerian's passion, and nothing substantial is ever expected of her. Valerian's wealth and elevated social position prohibit Margaret's friendship with Ondine, the one person in Valerian's life with whom she is comfortable. With her limited education and experience, she has nothing in common with wealthy socialites who would be appropriate companions. Margaret is isolated, and having a baby isolates her more. As Ondine surmises, Valerian kept Margaret stupid and idle, and Margaret punished him by sticking pins in his baby. "*Her* baby she loved" (240; emphasis added).

Margaret has no core of self and no culture. She belongs nowhere; she has no roots. Her unnatural mothering has alienated Michael, who apparently loves her but does not want to be near her. At Isle des Chevaliers she is merely a visitor in Valerian's domain. The solitude disquiets her—probably giving her too much time for reflection—and the island sun assaults her too-fair skin. In planning a special Christmas, Margaret attempts to create a cultural context for herself, but she fails. She wants a traditional Christmas with mother, father, son, and friends, a meal cooked by mother's own hands, a turkey, apple pies, and ollieballen, a Dutch bread. These are reassuring symbols of her place in the culture as she knows it. But these symbols are a hodgepodge, an amorphous collection that Margaret cannot assimilate as her own. Her failed Christmas plans suggest the incoherence of her life: Michael will never come home; there are no turkeys on the island; apples have to be imported at great expense, and moreover Margaret cannot cook, especially not a complicated Dutch bread. She is a "cultural orphan," and she has made Michael one as well. That explains his involvement in the struggle for African-American and Native American rights or in any struggle that brings him in proximity to people with cultural integrity.

However, Morrison suggests that the burden of guilt which Margaret has borne over the years has positioned her for forgiveness and triumph. That suffering has made her stronger than even she suspects. As Valerian is rendered weak by his seasons of innocence and is therefore in no condition to bear the burden of knowledge (when he hears about Michael's abuse, he collapses into a palsied stupor), Margaret emerges, burnished by the fires of suffering, redeemed and ready to take care of Valerian. She is no longer a visitor on Isle des Chevaliers as she settles into her role of organizer and caregiver. She appears natural and at peace, with her hair falling softly to her shoulders, free of its tortured, teased arrangement, and her face returning to familiarity without its made-up disguise. No longer in flight from herself, Margaret has a coherent identity, finally. And although it is nearly too late, she may be able to make friends with Ondine and rekindle their brief youthful intimacy. As women—their racial differences notwithstanding—they have a great deal in common, a special bond. Ondine kept Margaret's secret about Michael's abuse because it "was woman stuff" (207). She could not tell Margaret's husband or her own. They would not have understood, but Ondine does. She despises Margaret, judges her, becomes her "mother superior" (72), but only she, as a woman, understands and explains Margaret's transference of anger from Valerian to Michael. Morrison does not exonerate Margaret or minimize her crime. She merely counts it among the museum of horrible acts of which humans are capable. All of Morrison's characters are measured first against the yardstick of humanity and only after that by the rule of historical racial culture.

Sidney and Ondine, too, have interior viewpoints that layer their characterizations beyond thin stereotype. Morrison resists any urge to sanctify them as oppressed servants. They are not immune to the failings that afflict Margaret and Valerian. All are proud, arrogant; all usurp power where they can. Morrison does acknowledge social and racial differences, but these do not diminish the significance of their similarities; they do contribute, however, an abiding and remarkable tension threatening the tenuous boundaries of employee and employer.

Ondine reigns in the kitchen and larder, which are exclusively her domain. For thirty years Sidney has performed his duties as butler and personal attendant with elegant style and attention to detail. Together they administer the domestic chores of the house and yard. Their lives have been spent on the Streets (they have no friends, no children, no social activities outside of Valerian's house), but they do not feel exploited. Valerian's financial generosity has made groveling unnecessary, and thirty years of familiarity has softened the roles of master and servant. Indeed, in the end the roles are effectively reversed. In his palsied condition Valerian has lost most of his authority. Sidney, then, becomes not just Valerian's personal attendant, but like Margaret, a caregiver as well. In that capacity Sidney has authority, and he does not hesitate to use it.

In some sense Sidney and Ondine are as foreign to Isle des Chevaliers as Margaret and Valerian. They are self-described "Philadelphia Negroes" with a social status that sets them apart and above blacks from the South or from the Caribbean. These other blacks are not Negroes with a capital "N" but strangers, people whose ancestors had not successfully emulated white enterprise and industry as Sidney and Ondine's people had done in Philadelphia. They have proudly removed themselves from the category of "nigger," synonymous to them with uncultivated and, therefore, unworthy. Valerian is accurate in his fleeting estimation of them as smug and fraudulent in the proprietary pride they take in their employer's property, protecting it from "strangers" of the island. They acknowledge no bond and make no alliance with the other workers hired to maintain Valerian's orderly pace of life. Therese, who does the laundry, and Gideon, who handles yard chores, are merely faceless bodies to Sidney and Ondine. To them all the island women look alike, and one yardman (the name they assign to Gideon) is as shiftless and unfathomable as the next. When Valerian summarily fires Therese and Gideon for taking the Christmas apples, without first consulting Sidney and Ondine, the two question Valerian's behavior. It is, they feel, an affront to their position and a violation of their status. They pout and surreptitiously accuse a surprised Valerian of betrayal; only momentarily does his refusal to honor their claim that he owes them remind them that they are, after all, only hired help.

Sidney and Ondine's rank in the Street household is ambiguous at best. They are clearly more than servants, but how much more? Thirty years buys them privileges, but exactly what those privileges are is unclear. Their position is further complicated by the presence of Jadine, their twenty-four-year-old niece. As Sidney and Ondine's surrogate daughter, Jadine is by association with her family a member of the staff. She is also on the staff in deed, hired for a hiatus by Margaret as a companion. The two shop together, exercise together, and generally spend time in some mutual pursuit designed, it seems, to keep Margaret occupied. Jadine's "work" fuzzes the definitions of employer and friend: she takes meals with the Streets and is served as they are by her uncle; her bedroom is upstairs next to Margaret's, far from the servant's quarters Sidney and Ondine occupy near the kitchen. Jadine's anomalous relations are reflected in her quandary over an appropriate Christmas gift for Michael: "Should the—what?—social secretary buy a present for the son of her employer/patron? . . . A gift would embarrass him, probably, because he wouldn't have gotten one for her. Or would he? What had Margaret told him about the household? Even so, would he be offended by a gift from her, however modest?"(77).

Jadine is educated, beautiful, sophisticated, having more in common with Margaret than with Ondine or Sidney. They are her family, but she inhabits a world that is much larger than theirs, one that is closed to them. Yet, Jadine's privilege artificially inflates their status, deceiving them, for a time, into thinking they have more authority than they in fact have. In a crisis Ondine believes that "nothing can happen to us as long as she's [Jadine's] here" (87). They are mistaken, and it is not until Jadine abandons them to their fate with Valerian and returns to Paris that Sidney and Ondine take initiative in redefining their positions, contouring it to fit their desires.

Encouraged, no doubt, by Valerian's weakened condition and no longer willing to endure the limitations of serving only, the pair (Sidney especially) expand the old limits. In a final scene of the novel, in Valerian's greenhouse, Sidney enters, as is his custom, with a tray of food. Instead of leaving it as he usually does, he stays to handfeed Valerian and to assure him that "we'll give you the best of care. Just like we always done. That's something you ain't never got to worry about" (247). Sidney changes other parts of his normal routine as well. Over Valerian's objections he pours *himself* a glass of wine and, ignoring Valerian's talk of moving back to Philadelphia, decides that he and Ondine like the island's warmth and that moving is out of the question. In taking charge, Sidney unceremoniously revises his and Valerian's roles, and in response to such revision, Valerian can only half question, half mutter, "What's happening here? Something's happening here" (247).

Meanwhile, back in the kitchen, Ondine and Margaret are revising themselves. Despite the cloud of Margaret's crime hanging over them (or perhaps because of it: since only they knew about it, it bonds them), the women resume the laughter and camaraderie that Valerian had interrupted thirty years earlier because he objected to his wife's intimacy with the cook. Ondine and Sidney (and Margaret) are no longer subject to Valerian's power to preempt their lives. It is they who will take care of Valerian; they will, as Sidney promises, "give him the best of care." Morrison has, in her own words, "enormous respect"[5] for Sidney. Although, as she says, he may be considered "a good old Uncle Tom" by some, Morrison treats his commitment to family and work as a virtue. Indeed, Sidney and Ondine both are familiar as proud people, who, despite making the mistake of calculating their future in Valerian's commercial terms, are progenitors of an African-American tradition of pride in accomplishment.

Sidney endures, but Morrison severs the power that Valerian has drawn from his identity as a white male industrialist. Although he has not raised his own hand in abuse of that power, he has stood mute and blind to the systematic abuse of the inherent chauvinism of power in the world. His crime is willful innocence, and for that there is not reparation. Only those who have suffered the sin of crime (child abuse, pride, arrogance) are forgiven and redeemed.

Although the drama of white power and black power keeps Morrison occupied in *Tar Baby*, she is never far from the thematic concerns of black women: reconstructing themselves, expanding beyond conventional limitations. What price do women pay for the choices they make and for those they do not make? These and other themes inform Morrison's development of Jadine's character, which illuminates the opportunities and the dangers of black womanhood. Jadine is a new kind of character for Morrison. She is not the rebel, thwarting convention, that Sula is. She is not the mother-woman that Nel is, standing jealous guard over domesticity. She is not the culture bearer that Pilate is. Jadine is the modern women, a product of feminist ideology, mistress of the political and social system that ideology once opposed, embracing the values of that system: business enterprise, social connections, acquisition. With a graduate degree in art education and a career in high-fashion modeling, Jadine's determination to transcend the Baltimore housing project where she was born has been realized. The sealskin coat, made from the hides of "ninety baby seals" and sent as a Christmas present from her Parisian lover, represents just how far from her childhood she has moved. Jadine is seduced by the blackness of an expensive coat and not by the rhythms of black Africa. (Both she and the coat are superfluous on a warm Caribbean island that was once cultivated by the labor of black slaves.) The question Morrison poses, of course, is how far is too far from Baltimore and her cultural past? Jadine craves glamor, parties, and cities. In New York, for example, she feels at home. Its rhythms are familiar and delightful. To her it is a "black women's town . . . [where] the manifesto was simple: 'Talk shit. Take none'" (191). This is the language of working women all over New York whose confidence in themselves defines the city's pulsing beat. And Jadine numbers herself as one of them.

Although it is earned in some respects, Jadine's confidence in herself is fragile. It needs the reinforcement of numbers, the assurances of scores of city women like herself. Without them she is vulnerable to doubts. Without them she is threatened by her memory of an African woman in a Paris supermarket who spit at her. Jadine had been transfixed, like everyone else, by the woman's "transcendent beauty" (39) as she glided effortlessly, it seemed, through the market. She had represented womanhood itself; she was a "woman's woman," a "mother/sister/she" (39), as all definitions of womanliness found expression in her air of authority. The woman's insult to Jadine, then, had had the powerful effect of challenging Jadine's choices: her white boyfriend, her trendy girlfriends, her parties, her picture on the cover of *Elle,* the way she lived her life. Jadine hates the woman but cannot escape feeling "lonely and inauthentic" (40) because of her—except in New York.

Morrison points out the danger in Jadine's choices. The woman in the Paris market, whether consciously or not, calls attention to something that is missing in Jadine: she has no connection to her cultural past, and without it, Morrison suggests, she is vulnerable at the very least, and at most she is like the abused Michael, a cultural orphan. Sensing these dangers, Jadine flees Paris and retreats to Isle des Chevaliers, where Sidney and Ondine may offer protection. They are her people, her family, and she seeks them out "to touch bases, to sort out things before going ahead with, with, with anything" (41). But the island offers her no refuge. It is not home and Sidney and Ondine are only surrogate parents. She has never really lived with them except during summers spent at Valerian's house, and she does not really value their opinions. Jadine's position in the household as Margaret's employee/friend/guest underscores these ambiguities.

Without ancestors to point the way, Jadine may never discover the path to black womanhood. Like Margaret she will have no traditions and will have to find a way to live with her feelings of inauthenticity. When it is too late, Ondine tries to guide Jadine, but all that she is really able to do is express regrets:

> Jadine, a girl has got to be a daughter first. She have to learn that. And if she never learns how to be a daughter, she can't never learn how to be a woman. I mean a real woman: a woman good enough for a child; good enough for a man—good enough for the respect of other women. Now you didn't have a mother long enough to learn much about it and I thought I was doing right by sending you to all them schools and so I never told you it and I should have. You don't need your own natural mother to be a daughter.

All you need is to feel a certain way, a certain careful way about people older
than you are. . . . A daughter is a woman that cares about where she come
from and takes care of them that took care of her. (242)

In their own pride and arrogance, Sidney and Ondine have tacitly encouraged their niece's cultural disconnection as a sign of her and their
success. They liked her living in Paris; they liked her acceptance by their
employer. But they had not heeded the price of such acceptance: someone
who is alienated from black culture, someone who prefers Chagall to Entuma
masks, a woman who does not know how to be a respectful daughter.
Being black, Morrison suggests, is not only a matter of genetics; it is also a
matter of culture. Gideon is wrong when he says it's hard for Jadine to
choose blackness because she is a "yella" and therefore more white than
black. Jadine does not choose blackness because, as Ondine knows, she has
never learned what it is; she has not been acculturated. As Morrison notes
in *Song of Solomon,* without a chorus of mamas and aunts tending her, a
black woman may easily loose her way.

Jadine has not learned the things she needs to know to be the "real
woman" that Ondine describes. She has never known the "ancient properties" of black womanhood. Morrison observes, with regret, this aspect of
her character's failings when Jadine falls into a tar pit on Isle des Chevaliers. Surrounded by aged trees whose long, mossy growths assume mythic
proportions, Jadine rejects the trees' maternal delight in her return to them.
As she struggles to free herself, they realize that she is not "a runaway child
. . . restored to them" (157). She does not acknowledge her link to their
"exceptional femaleness" (157). She does not know "as they did that the
first world of the world had been built with their sacred properties; that
they alone could hold together the stones of pyramids and rushes of Moses's
crib" (157). They marvel at her "desperate struggle . . . to be something
other than they were" (157). She does not know, Morrison rebukes, her
place in their history, which is the history of black womanhood, which is
"as old as the hills."

Jadine rejects the tree women just as she does the night women who
crowd into her room and keep her awake by revealing their breasts. They
are joined by the African woman in the Paris market, who shows "her three
big eggs" (222), symbols of female fertility. These are all the women who
have not tried to escape their history. They—her mother, Ondine, Therese,
the living, and the dead—come not so much to accuse as to persuade her
to follow. These visions are manifestations of Jadine's divided self: she wants
to live as a woman of the world, inventing herself as she goes, not tethered

to the past, but some part of her needs tradition. Without it her identity is shifting, always in progress; she will never know who she is. Jadine, however, refuses to be initiated into the cult of black womanhood by the night women. She challenges the women's invasion by declaring that she, too, has breasts. When that does not work, she decides to deconstruct the image, "slice it open and see what lay in its belly" (225). She tells herself that the "women looked awful: . . . onion heels, potbellies, hair surrendered to rags and braids. And the breasts they thrust at her like weapons were soft, loose bags closed at the tip . . ." (225). Jadine hopes to outdistance the women by synchronizing her pace to the speed of cities like Paris and New York. In these places she can replace the women with friends whose names— Dawn, Aisha, Felicite, Betty—like her own, are not cultural throwbacks but emblems of finesse and success.

Jadine's foil in the novel is Son Green. If she is in retreat from black culture, he embodies its deepest currents. On Isle des Chevaliers, with its oozing, rich association to Africa and the Caribbean, Jadine feels misplaced even as Son is easily at home. From the moment he jumps ship, landing feet first in the "soft and warm" (1) island sea, emerging reborn from the "water that heaved and pulsed in the ammonia-scented air" (2), Son is embraced by the water-lady as one of her own. "His skin blended well with the dark [night] water" (1). Later, on the island, unwashed and half-starved, he is identified with the rest of nature, poised to [re]claim L'Arbe de la Croix, return it to precolonial wildness, and spoil the superficial harmony (that Jadine labors diligently to maintain) of its residents. Once inside the house, he does just that.

William "Son" Green is a specimen of Morrison's traveling man. He is not a chronic wanderer by nature and by choice as are Ajax and Cholly, "dangerously free" to refuse responsibility for anyone but themselves. Killing his wife by running his car into the bedroom where she is sleeping with her thirteen-year-old lover makes him a fugitive. But for that he would probably have remained at home in Eloe, Florida. Once on the run, he is indistinguishable, for a time, from the dangerous ones, the "international legion of day laborers" who refused "to equate work with life" (143). By nature, however, Son is most like Milkman at the end of his journey to self-knowledge. Milkman discovers the self that Son already knows. Son is rooted in cultural pride; his values are spiritual. He refuses the rituals of success; he refuses "to live in the world their way" (148).

For a time Son is the only one at L'Arbe de la Croix with so honest a representation of himself in the world. But in response to his trespass in

Margaret's closet, everyone—Margaret, Valerian, Sidney, Ondine, Jadine—
is eventually unmasked, forced to reveal and confront his or her crimes and
deceptions. For as Morrison reveals, the Tar Baby tale seems to her to be
about masks, and in her novel all the major characters except Son wear
them. His "most effective mask," she says, "is none."[6] At the dinner table,
then, on Christmas Day, Son, washed and fed, presides at the other characters' unveiling. Sidney and Ondine are the first to lift the edges of their
facade as sovereigns in the household. For most of their adult lives, the two
have been Valerian's loyal employees. That loyalty has been nourished by
an understanding that Valerian appreciates not only their fidelity, but their
authority as well. When Valerian fires Therese and Gideon without Sidney's
and Ondine's knowledge, their identities are called into question. "I may
be a cook," Ondine reminds Valerian, "but I'm a person too" (178). The
hypocrisy of the pair's position is underscored by the Christmas scene: cook
and butler seated at dinner as guests, dressed in their finest clothes, feeling
betrayed by their employer, whom they now realize sees them (despite
their presence at his table) merely as the help. Having been forced to remove half of her mask, Ondine rips off the remainder. If, indeed, she has
no authority, then her loyalty has gone unrewarded, and she is not obliged
to remain so. Feeling a reckless liberty and righteous indignation, Ondine,
in effect, reaches across the dinner table to rip away Margaret's mask: Margaret is not the sensitive, inspired mother she believes herself to be; she is a
"white freak!" a "baby killer!" who "stuck pins in his [Michael's] behind.
Burned him with cigarettes" (179). At first Margaret retreats from Ondine's
accusations, but then, like Ondine, she feels an unaccustomed liberation
without her mask. She welcomes "the wonderful relief of public humiliation, the solid security of the pillory . . ."(202).

For Margaret, Ondine, and Sidney, Son merely witnesses the unmask-
ing; for Valerian and Jadine, he precipitates it. They hide more and therefore have more to reveal. Son will not permit Valerian, for example, to
continue parading the mantle of fair, benevolent employer. He reminds
Valerian that he is not entitled to any moral outrage over the apples Therese
and Gideon took. Valerian merely paid for the fruit. He had not "row[ed]
eighteen miles to bring them here. They did" (177). Now two people
would starve so Margaret "could play American mama and fool around in
the kitchen" (177). Stunned by Son's brutal assessment, Valerian no longer
perceives himself to be tolerantly amused. He stands exposed as an arrogant colonialist, successor to the French horsemen who once invaded the

island and changed its landscape. As Son speaks, "Somewhere in the back of Valerian's mind one hundred French chevaliers were roaming the hills on horses. Their swords were in their scabbards, and their epaulets glittered in the sun. Backs straight, shoulders high—alert but restful in the security of the Napoleonic Code" (177). In anger Valerian struggles to reconstruct the identity he has artfully created. He orders Son to leave L'Arbe de la Croix, and when Son refuses, Valerian declares in disbelief to his wife: "I am being questioned by these people, as if, as if I *could* be called into question" (177).

At the moment Valerian is reconstructing his history with the image of conquering French horsemen, Son is constructing his own history with images of African horsemen and precolonial time on the island:

> Somewhere in the back of Son's mind one hundred black men on one hundred unshod horses rode blind and naked through hills and had done so for hundreds of years. They knew the rain forest when it was a rain forest, they knew where the river began, where the roots twisted above the ground; they knew all there was to know about the island and had not even seen it. They had floated in strange waters blind, but they were still there racing each other for sport in the hills behind this white man's house. (177)

Son's moral authority flows from these slaves and descendants of slaves. It is they and he who must inherit the earth and not the Valerian Streets of the industrial world. That is the disturbing message that Son brings to everyone and especially to Jadine. She, Son thinks, is too available to do Valerian's bidding. At the dinner table it is she who keeps the assembly going smoothly "quietly chastising everybody," "agreeing with Valerian" (176). She has become too much like a "little white girl" (103), he believes, and he is compelled to "insert his own dreams [of fat black ladies in white dresses and men in magenta slacks on street corners] into her . . . to breathe into her the smell of tar and its shiny consistency" (102).

It is Jadine, however, who alters Son's dreams. As a black woman living in a social world that is mostly white, Jadine is the tar baby of the novel's title. Like the tar baby of the Uncle Remus tales that the farmer uses to entrap Br'er Rabbit, Jadine is mistaken by Son, Morrison's Br'er Rabbit for something she is not. In spite of her upscale lifestyle and extraordinary beauty, he thinks she is a variety of the women he has known. These were strong women who faced and usually survived their hard lives in rural Eloe:

Before Francine was attacked by dogs, she gave him ten points on the court and still beat him. . . . Cheyenne was driving a beat-up old truck at age nine, four years before he could even shift gears, and she could drop a pheasant like an Indian. His mother's memory was kept alive by those who remembered how she roped horses when she was a girl. His grandmother built a whole cowshed with only Rosa to help. . . . Anybody who thought women were inferior didn't come out of north Florida. (231)

In comparison, Son thinks "the black girls in New York City were crying and their men were looking neither to the right nor to the left" (185). Son sees their gray and colorless faces veiled in heavy plum lipstick. They are a whole new race of people with no ancestors, no past, no traditions. He wonders where the old people are. There are no cultural antecedents like Therese and Gideon in New York. And there are no children, laughing and spontaneous. Without ancestry and progeny, without a past and a future, the crying girls have nothing in common with the women of Eloe, the tree women on Isle des Chevaliers, the night women, or the African woman in the Paris market. By the time Son realizes that Jadine is of the New York variety of black woman whose strength lay in the spasms of industry and efficiency with which she handily negotiates "the First Cities of the world" (230), it is too late for him to pull back. Like Br'er Rabbit he is stuck fast.

Valerian, associated as he is with the greenhouse, is no doubt the farmer who creates tar baby Jadine. He has paid for her education, influenced her values, and generally made her style of living possible. He is even expected to underwrite any future business enterprises Jadine may pursue. Son, as Br'er Rabbit, is trickster and thief who, when he is hungry, steals Valerian's food. But more significant, he is Valerian's antithesis; he threatens Valerian's peace of mind and opposes his material values. As Valerian's protégée, the dangerously attractive Jadine seduces Son into exchanging his African worldview for her (and Valerian's) Western view. At first Son resists; he perceives Jadine as a "tar baby side-of-the-road whore tramp" (189), but he believes he can change that. Instead, he is the one transformed, willing to do "whatever she wants" (235). Seeing through Jadine's eyes the pictures of places and people that he had loved in Eloe, "that used to comfort him so, used to reside with him, in him like royalty in his veins," (253) changes Son. These no longer matter. He willingly replaces his dreams of community and fraternity with Jadine's dreams of getting ahead and getting over. Unlike Br'er Rabbit, Son does not want to escape; he is "stuck in it and revolted by the possibility of being freed" (259) even if that means living "in the garden of some other white people house" (263). In surrender he abandons Eloe and all that he believes about the authority and purity of blackness.

In his present condition only Therese has the power to release Son and restore his faith in home. When Son entreats her to take him across the bay to Isle des Chevaliers so that he can find Jadine and acquiesce, Therese takes him instead to join the blind African horsemen who are said to have been riding the hills for more than a century. Forget Jadine, Therese advises. "There is nothing in her parts for you. She has forgotten her ancient properties" (263). Therese intervenes to redirect Son away from a foreigner's garden to his own briar patch on the far side of Isle des Chevaliers, where the ancestors await. In the final lines of text—"Lickety-split. Looking neither to the left nor to the right. Lickety-split. Lickety-split. Lickety-lickety-lickety-split,"—Morrison calls attention to the rabbit's escape.

The tar baby theme is not as simple as this analysis suggests. Morrison layers meaning to reflect the complex nature of experience. As flesh and blood woman Jadine has choices. She is not an inanimate tool subject to be molded by Valerian's society: she *chooses* not to be aligned with the "deep dark" (157) tar of the island earth, the ancient properties of the swamp women, the substance of all the black women who have nurtured Son and who generate the smell of tar that he attempts to breathe into Jadine's dreams (102). Jadine eschews the deep dark for the shallow veneer.

Although it may seem so, Morrison is not choosing sides. She renders the difficulties of each point of view and the heartrending consequences for both characters. Jadine

> thought she was rescuing him from the night women who wanted him for themselves, wanted him feeling superior in a cradle, deferring to him; wanted her to settle for wifely competence when she could be almighty, to settle for fertility rather than originality, nurturing instead of building. He thought he was rescuing her from Valerian, meaning *them*, the aliens, the people who in a mere three hundred years had killed a world millions of years old. . . . Each was pulling the other away from the maw of hell. . . . Each knew the world as it was meant or ought to be. (231–32)

Morrison acknowledges the bitter truth of each accusation and the awful necessity of each demand. Perhaps Son (as the infantile appellation implies) has been suckled too long by the night women with their magical breasts. Perhaps in clinging to Eloe, he is romanticizing the past and home which to him has always been a "place that was presided over by wide black women . . ." (144). When Therese calls him "small boy" and leads him back in time to the African horsemen and away from a future with Jadine, it is she and not Son who determines his direction. Even to the end he is the suckled. Perhaps Jadine is right when she urges Son to let go, when she advises "there is nothing any of us can do about the past but make our own lives better. . . . That is the only revenge, for us to get over" (234). Morrison acknowledges this dilemma of the modern woman, thrust into the tiresome either/or scenario: either become a wife and mother or take on the world of work-for-pay "as though," Morrison says, "you can't do two things or do one and then stop it and go do something else."[7] Jadine feels pressed to choose, and she does. In Paris, away from Son, is financial success and personal independence. In leaving Son, she has avoided "wifely competence" and "fertility" (231), and she has "refused to be broken in the big ugly hands of any man" (237). In flight she feels "lean and male" (237). Her fate is not that of the unspayed passive bitch "standing quietly under the paws of a male" (250). In her world "A grown woman did not need safety or its dreams. She *was* the safety she longed for" (250).

In this profile Jadine seems akin to Sula, who refuses to care more about a man than she does herself. And like Sula, Jadine rejects the role of nurturer; neither values community traditions and rituals that seem to abridge the individual's freedoms. With Sula, however, Morrison confines her scope to the tension between the community and the rebel in its midst. There, she is concerned with how each finds an uneasy acceptance of the other. With Jadine, Morrison enlarges her concern from matters of self-sufficiency to grander matters of sexual equality. Sula is a pariah who remains within the community; Jadine is a feminist who lives outside. And she is a feminist "without . . . concern for social justice" (78),[8] connected as she is with Valerian and his rape of the earth and its people.

There is little doubt that Jadine has moved too far from the village; she has never found her ancient properties. In getting over, she has sidestepped her place in the line of history. Neither daughter nor mother, she has heedlessly severed her link to the past and to the future of black womanhood. In dedicating *Tar Baby* to her grandmother, mother, aunts, and sister, "all of whom knew their true and ancient properties," Morrison implies the importance of that link. Morrison does not find fault with Jadine's ambitions. Jadine's fault is in not building on the strength of those who have preceded her, in accepting the either/or interpretation of her choices. Morrison believes that no one should be asked to make a choice between a home and a career. "Why not have both? It's all possible. Like women doing nine things since the beginning and getting to the end of the row at the same time."[9] Perhaps Jadine is right in admiring the kick-ass black women taking charge in New York. But Son is also right in seeing the price they have paid for such power; they have sacrificed the ancestors and the children. Jadine and Son each has a partial answer. "One had a past, the other a future and each one bore the culture to save the race in his hands" (232).

Tar Baby is a fable for these modern times when the old stories are unfamiliar to a recent generation that needs to learn its lessons as much, if not more, than the previous generations. As a paradigm of black/white relations, the tale of a wily rabbit outwitting an unsuspecting farmer has, for blacks, as far back as slavery, confirmed their status as shrewd survivors. Morrison updates the tale, revises it to accommodate her form and to reflect her themes. Since, as she reminds, "We don't live in places where we can hear those stories anymore, a way to get "new information" out must be discovered.[10] In Morrison's estimation the novel is the best conduit of such information. In this context, "the novel is needed by African Americans now in a way that it was not needed before"[11] to identify the pitfalls of contemporary life for those who are running from the past.

Notes

1. Robert G. O'Meally, "Review of *Tar Baby*," *Callaloo* (Feb.–Oct. 1981): 193.

2. Gloria Naylor and Toni Morrison, "A Conversation," *Southern Review* 21 (1985): 581.

3. Toni Morrison, *Tar Baby* (New York: Alfred A. Knopf, 1981) 7. Subsequent references will appear in parentheses in the text.

4. Terry Otten, *The Crime of Innocence in the Fiction of Toni Morrison* (Columbia: University of Missouri, 1989) 4–5.

5. Nellie Y. McKay, "An Interview with Toni Morrison," *Contemporary Literature* 24 (Winter 1983): 413–29. Rpt. in *Toni Morrison: Critical Perspectives Past and Present*, ed. Henry Louis Gates, Jr., and K. A. Appiah (New York: Amistad, 1993) 405.

6. Toni Morrison, "Unspeakable Things Unspoken: The Afro-American Presence in American Literature," *Michigan Quarterly Review* 28 (Winter 1989): 30.

7. Naylor and Morrison 573.

8. Barbara Christian, "The Concept of Class in the Novels of Toni Morrison," *Black Feminist Criticism* (New York: Pergamon Press, 1985) 79.

9. Naylor and Morrison 575.

10. Toni Morrison, "Rootedness: The Ancestor as Foundation," *Black Women Writers 1950–1980,* ed. Marie Evans (New York: Doubleday, 1984) 340.

11. Morrison, "Rootedness" 340.

5

REMEMBERING THE "DISREMEMBERED"

BELOVED

When *Tar Baby* was finished, Morrison expected to stop writing novels. After four successful performances she was, for a time, without the urgent need to say something that had not been said before. She no longer had a messianic will to tell about people that only she knew, in a way that only she could. In 1974, at the time of her first novel, she was strongly convinced that no one "is going to see what I saw which was this complex poetic life. . . . And no one is going to write from the inside with that kind of gentleness. . . ."[1] A decade later Morrison perceived the gap between the black experience and the representation of that experience to be closing. A second renaissance in black literary arts had redressed the paucity of books about women's lives. She could "look at the work . . . and find . . . [herself] properly spoken of in it."[2] Ironically, in this milieu of productivity and creative possibility, Morrison decided not to write anymore, feeling relieved perhaps of the responsibility to shape her special vision of black culture since her subject matter, heretofore sporadically explored, was being confidently, sensitively, and consistently mined by her contemporaries. Morrison could rest, so to speak.

Her hiatus from writing was short-lived. Three years after *Tar Baby*, *Beloved* was published. The old and by now familiar feeling of creating a story unique to her sensibilities had returned. Once more she felt responsible for delineating characters that only she knew, as if she "had the direct line . . . [and] was the receiver of all this information."[3] This time she was "obsessed by two or three little fragments of stories" of extraordinary women. Morrison recalls that

> One was a newspaper clipping about a woman named Margaret Garner in 1851. It said that the Abolitionists made a great deal out of her case because she had escaped from Kentucky, I think, with her four children. She lived in a little neighborhood just outside of Cincinnati and she had killed her children. She succeeded in killing one; she tried to kill two others. She hit them in the head with a shovel and they were wounded, but they didn't die. And there was a smaller one that she had at her breast. The interesting thing, in addition to that, was the interview that she gave. She was a young woman. In the inked pictures of her she seemed a very quiet, very serene-looking woman and everyone who interviewed her remarked about her serenity and tranquility. She said, "I will not let those children live how I lived." She had run off into a little woodshed right outside her house to kill them because she had been caught as a fugitive. And she had made up her mind that they would not suffer the way she had and it was better for them to die. And her mother-in-law was in the house at the same time and she said, "I watched her and I neither encouraged her nor discouraged her." They put her in a jail for a while and I'm not even sure what the denouement is of her story. But that moment, that decision was a piece, a tail of something that was always around, and it didn't get clear for me until I was thinking of another story that I had read in a book that Camille Billops published, a collection of pictures by Van der Zee, called *The Harlem Book of the Dead*.[4]

Van der Zee narrates each photograph, giving his subjects stories and contexts. One photograph that intrigued Morrison featured an eighteen-year-old girl lying in a coffin. According to the photographer, the girl had slumped to the floor at a party. When people around her asked what happened, she would only say "I'll tell you tomorrow." The girl died, apparently shot by a jealous lover who had entered the party with a gun and a silencer. Of course, the girl knew this, but she kept her story until her lover could escape. She cared for him so much that she could, with one supreme act, forgive him for her murder and protect him from punishment.

This girl's and Margaret Garner's stories seemed to Morrison essentially related to each other. Both women, in Morrison's words, "sabotage[d]" themselves, "displace[d]" themselves for people they loved. Morrison's original plan for *Beloved*, then, was to cement the two stories with a single donnée. Margaret Garner's story would be refracted by the Harlem girl's story when Garner's dead daughter is reincarnated in this life, perhaps as the eighteen-year-old. Morrison explains:

I just imagined her [Garner's daughter] remembering what happened to her, being someplace else and returning, knowing what happened to her. And I call her Beloved so that I can filter all these confrontations and questions that she has in that situation, which is 1851, and then to extend her life, you know, her search, her quest, all the way through as long as I care to go, into the [nineteen-]twenties where it switches to this other girl. Therefore, I have a New York uptown-Harlem milieu in which to put this love story, but Beloved will be there also.[5]

Morrison's plans for weaving the "fragments" into a single continuous pattern were never completed. At some point during its development, *Beloved* became the contemporary slave narrative that it is, opening and closing on Sethe, the fictionalized Margaret Garner. Intermittently intervening are the memories that Morrison planned for Beloved, but these never range beyond 1851 to encompass a dead girl in Harlem. That girl would be the subject of Morrison's latest novel, *Jazz*, which is set in 1920s New York. (The two novels are part of a planned trilogy.)

Despite revisions in the first blueprint, Morrison does retain in *Beloved* her concern with a woman's extraordinary capacity for love and sacrifice. Sethe does kill her two-year-old daughter, and she does attempt to kill the other three children before she is stopped, because she wants to place them "where no one could hurt them . . . where they would be safe."[6] This concept of love and safety as motivation for infanticide is a familiar inversion of conventional thinking in Morrison's work. As no one else can, Morrison renders the terrible moment with perfect reason and clarity. Practiced Morrison readers may phrase a note of sorrow for the painful inevitability of things, but they never ask why. The feeble question "what she go and do that for?" (150) is left to the sadistic slavemaster, Schoolteacher, and his nephews. (Paul D and the black community ostracize Sethe but not because they cannot understand why she acts; they question her right to do so.) These same people take false comfort in easy explanations: Sethe lost her reason because she couldn't take a little "mishandle[ing]" (150).

But Morrison's queries in *Beloved* are not about what Sethe does or why. These answers are available to anyone with knowledge of slavery. Morrison asks who. Who is the woman capable of making such a choice? Who is the woman with such audacity? In her search for Sethe, Morrison returns to the first flashes of insight stirred by the "fragments": Sethe is the kind of woman who "loved something other than herself so much, she has placed all of the value of her life in something outside herself" in her children.[7]

Morrison renders Sethe, then, almost completely as mother—not in any predictably pejorative meaning of the role, but as a woman whose love for her children has absolutely no limits in spite of slavery, which subverts all relationships and kinships. Sethe, like many children born into slavery, had not known her own mother. Raised communally by the plantation's wet nurse (after two weeks with her mother), she had no rights to the scared woman who had briefly and surreptitiously identified herself as Sethe's mother and who was later hanged. At Sweet Home, Sethe's children had fared better; they had a mother and a father. The Garners had created the illusion of security for their slaves, and through diligence and persistence Sethe managed to mother her children and protect them from environmental dangers: fire, the well, animals. When Garner dies and Schoolteacher takes over, the illusion is shattered, and Sethe is forced to face a brutal reality of slavery: her children do not belong to her. They are property, subject to be sold, traded, raped, beaten, disposed of. In order to make them safe, she and they would have to escape. And they do. First the children run, and later she, pregnant with a baby that she delivers in route to freedom.

Escape is Sethe's emphatic rejection of slavery's power to circumscribe her motherhood. Barefoot, bleeding, hungry, exhausted, disoriented, Sethe struggles to reach Ohio, not so much to save her own life, but "the life of her children's mother" (30). Only she has milk enough in her breasts for her two-year-old, who had gone ahead, and for her newborn. Sethe suffers with the knowledge that "little whitebabies got it [her mother's milk] first" (200) and she got what was left. She "knows what it is to be without the milk that belongs to you; to have to fight and holler for it, and to have so little left" (200). By the time she reaches her babies, she will have "milk enough for all" (100). In Ohio, under the expert care of her mother-in-law, Baby Suggs, Sethe begins to claim herself and her children. She nurses the baby girls and kisses the boys from "the tops of their heads [to] their tight round bellies" (94). For twenty-eight days—the cycle of preparation a woman's body needs to begin a new life—Sethe's motherlove is unrestrained. She remembers that her love felt "good and right . . . and when I stretched out my arms all my children could get in between. I was *that* wide. Look like I loved em more after I got here. Or maybe I couldn't love em proper in Kentucky because they wasn't mine to love" (162).

When Schoolteacher (named, according to Morrison, to reflect the scholarly way in which racism was pursued in theology and in biology in the Darwinian theory of evolution),[8] his nephew, and the sheriff enter Baby

Suggs's yard to reclaim Sethe and, worse, to take her children back into slavery, Sethe revolts. In an instant she is transported back to the brutal beating she endured in the hours before her escape and to her deepest violation: being suckled by Schoolteacher's nephews, being "handled" (200) as if she were a goat, being robbed of the milk that belonged to her babies. Stirred by her memories, Sethe resolves that "nobody will ever get my milk no more except my children" (200). Threatened by Schoolteacher's arrival, she collects "every bit of life she had made, all the parts of her that were precious and fine and beautiful" (163) and carries them to the woodshed. Finally, they would all be "over there. Outside this place, where they would be safe" (163).[9]

Sethe's action places her outside the Ohio community of former slaves. She becomes one of Morrison's outlaw characters—much like Sula and Pilate (but unlike them also)—in conflict with communal values. After the woodshed she must give up Baby Suggs's healing care, and all ties of friendship that developed for twenty-eight days are severed by those who fear her determination. They "understand Sethe's rage . . . but not her reaction to it . . ." (256). They had not responded to their own unspeakable and unforgivable insults so outrageously. Ella had survived the sexual sadism of her master and his son who had taken turns with her. Stamp Paid had steeled himself to the rage he felt when he had "handed over his wife to his master's son" (184). For not killing the master, himself, or his wife he had stamped any debt he or any slave owed to the institution as paid. Like Stamp and Ella, Baby Suggs, too, had outlived an intolerable life. She neither condones nor condemns Sethe, but unlike her daughter-in-law, she had learned not to mourn the seven children she had borne but not been allowed to keep. Like the others she understood the "nastiness of life" (23). Slavery made love risky, even dangerous according to Paul D, the last of the Sweet Home men, "especially if it was her [a woman's] children she had settled on to love. The best thing, he knew, was to love just a little bit; everything, just a little bit, so when they broke its back, or shoved it in a croaker sack, well, maybe you'd have a little love left over for the next one" (45). Sethe, however, does not love so timidly. She refutes any compromise of her maternity. She had "birthed" them; "got em out" and "it felt good" (162). She would not see them returned to slavery. "The best thing she was, was her children. Whites might dirty *her* all right, but not her best thing, her beautiful, magical best thing—the part of her that was clean" (251). Her job was keeping them away from what she knew was terrible. "I did that," she declares.

Sethe's exercise of power is, in effect, a declaration of independence from an unsympathetic community, and the ensuing clash informs a latent tension in the novel that is unresolved until the final pages. Community finds expression as traits of character in Morrison's novels. Its values and beliefs shape the background against which the individual's behavior is assessed and defined. As a repository of cultural traditions, the community is usually necessary to the individual's wholeness and identity, and those who do not embrace it are incomplete as is Jadine in *Tar Baby*. But sometimes the role of community is not so easily justified. In such instances its function as cultural arbiter is tainted by a smugness and pettiness which the individual who would be free is compelled to resist—as with Sula. The case is similar in *Beloved*, when the community abridges its natural function through spite, jealousy, and meanness. Before Sethe arrives in Ohio, the black community maintains the integrity of its purpose with Baby Suggs at its moral core. Her house, 124 Bluestone, was the gathering place, the community center. There, people came to discuss "the true meaning of the Fugitive Bill, the Settlement Fee, God's Ways, and Negro pews; antislavery, manumission, skin voting, Republicans, Dred Scott, book learning, Sojourner's highwheeled buggy, the Colored Ladies of Delaware, Ohio, and the other weighty issues" (173) that concerned them. In the clearing behind the house, Baby Suggs taught the people to dance, to laugh, and to love themselves. In this setting for twenty-eight days Sethe had "women friends, a mother-in-law, and all her children together" (173). When these same people betray Baby Suggs and her family by failing to warn of what they instinctively know is trouble when white men come to town asking questions, the community fails its obligation to the individual. Baby Suggs is mortally disillusioned. She abandons her ministry of love and slowly gives up life. "To belong to a community of other free Negroes—to love and be loved by them, to counsel and be counselled, protect and be protected, feed and be fed—and then to have that community step back and hold itself at a distance—well, it could wear out even a Baby Suggs, holy" (177).

Like the individuals that comprise it, the community is collectively subject to character flaws: envy of Baby Suggs's generosity and of Sethe's youth and deftness flowers into meanness. After holding themselves at a distance and not warning Sethe, people in the community gather but do not raise their voices in the customary unifying ceremony of song when Sethe is taken to jail. Later they rumor doubts about Sethe's past: did she really escape from slavery in her condition? Was Baby Suggs's son really the father of her children? Ten years later, after Baby Suggs's funeral, they congregate in the yard, eating the food they brought and leaving Sethe's untouched. After that time no one visits 124, and rankled by her independence and self-sufficiency, "Just about everybody in town was longing for Sethe to come on difficult times" (171). For nearly two decades Sethe and Denver (and later Paul D) are left to themselves, solitary figures living at the edge of the community.

Morrison does not censure or judge the community for its treatment of Sethe. Most crimes in her fictional world are redeemable. Despite its coldness, for example, the community does not entirely expel Sethe, and in the end, when she is haunted by the ghost of her daughter and is no longer self-supporting, it reclaims her as its own.

In the interim Morrison explicates the tension between Sethe and her neighbors to illuminate Sethe's character: she is impenitent and tough. She refuses to seek the community's approval, and each act of their disapproval evokes a corresponding defiance from Sethe. They hold themselves distant when Schoolteacher comes; Sethe holds herself aloof from the crowd when she is taken to jail and remains aloof when she is released. Many years later, when Baby Suggs dies, they set up tables of food in the yard because no one will enter the house; Sethe will not attend the funeral service and will not join in their singing at the graveside. Back in the yard of 124, they do not eat Sethe's food, and she does not touch theirs. Nearly a month of fellowship is followed by nearly twenty years of alienation. The uncommunal action of holding back begets an unbroken pattern of mutual spurns. The community erred, Sethe rebuked it, and neither will relent.

These social dynamics are different from those in *Tar Baby*. The earlier novel dissects Morrison's abiding interest in the individual's initiation to mythic and folk culture in the community. Without initiation, Morrison warns, self-knowledge is imperfect. The communities (Eloe, Florida, and Isle des Chevaliers) in *Tar Baby* do not hold themselves back; they strive to assimilate Jadine into cultures of black womanhood. In choosing to live in Paris, however, Jadine cuts herself off from black people and in doing so deprives herself of an identity as black woman. She may be, as she stubbornly asserts, self-dependent, but without assimilating historical culture, she is fundamentally incomplete. This is the dilemma of contemporary life. Community dynamics in *Beloved* are not so apocryphal. In *Beloved*, with its 1850s setting, Morrison is not, as she was in *Tar Baby*, forewarning of the dire consequences of a failure by the individual to be acculturated by the community. Sethe is not in danger, as Jadine is, of losing her identity as black woman (she is endeavoring to *make* an identity as black woman).

Indeed, in denying historical identity, Jadine, in effect, denies her link to Sethe and her struggle. Sethe's conflict with her neighbors is virulent but not as lethal as Jadine's. Sethe continues in the community (even if on the periphery) and is reconnected with it when the women save her from the child ghost who threatens to replace Sethe's life with its own. Sethe knows, as Jadine does not, that her fight is not with these people with whom she has so much suffering in common. Her struggle is against Schoolteacher, his nephews, and the system which enslaves, degrades, and defines.

In Morrison's work Sethe is the prototypical womanist.[10] In the time line of Morrison's novels, she is the first of Morrison's women to demand the privilege of defining herself. Contemporary women like Jadine are expected to make these demands, but Morrison demonstrates that these recent combatants owe much to their predecessors. The particular demands have changed—Jadine sees motherhood as inhibiting, and Sethe sees it as necessary—but the essential struggle for self-definition is the same. Sethe, like her mother, Baby Suggs, and all slave women, can never be wife and mother. She is biologically female, and she is a breeder, but she is exempt from all ideological considerations as woman. She is no more than a cow or goat subject to "milking" like any other beast. Schoolteacher and his pupils confirm these categories by compiling a list of Sethe's animal characteristics for study and evaluation. Sethe resists this nonhuman suborder by proving herself capable of thinking for herself and by insisting upon the right to determine her own and her children's fates in life and in death. She will not have them liable to Schoolteacher's demeaning measurements of their "animal" qualities. Sethe had "felt what it felt like and nobody walking or stretched out" was going to make her children feel it too (203). Sethe acts, then, alone—sending her children along the underground a week before she escapes. Morrison calls attention to the magnitude of Sethe's defiance by accenting her aloneness. All the men at Sweet Home who were supposed to run away together and take Sethe and the children are either dead or in chains. Six-O was burned alive, one Paul had been sold, two killed, and Paul D was locked in the barn with a bit in his mouth. Halle, Sethe's "husband," unable to rescue his wife from the vile nephews who take her milk, cracks under the strain and sits near the butter churn, spreading creamy fat over his face. Sethe takes no refuge in insanity:

> Other people went crazy. . . . Other people's brains stopped, turned around and went on to something new, which is what must have happened to Halle. And how sweet that would have been: the two of them back by the milk shed, squatting by the churn, smashing cold, lumpy butter into their

faces with not a care in the world. . . . But her three children were chewing sugar teat under a blanket on their way to Ohio and no butter play would change that. (70)

For Sethe, the duties of motherhood are not dissolved by mental disarrangements. Sethe savors the size of her accomplishment:

> I did it. I got us all out. Without Halle too. Up till then it was the only thing I ever did on my own. Decided. And it came off right, like it was supposed to. . . . Each and every one of my babies and me too. I birthed them and I got em out and it wasn't no accident. I did that. I had help, of course, lots of that, but still it was me doing it; me saying. *Go on,* and *now.* Me having to look out. Me using my own head. (162)

Schoolteacher's arrival threatens to reduce Sethe again to a list of parts and jeopardizes her self-confidence. But more than these dangers, Schoolteacher's insistent presence forces Sethe to stake her claim as a mother who is capable of defending her children's lives.

That responsibility is abridged only once. Briefly, Sethe had placed "the responsibility for her breasts . . . in somebody else's hands" (18); Paul D had relieved her of their burden. For the first time since the woodshed, she could "trust things and remember things because the last of the Sweet Home men was there to catch her if she sank" (18). Sethe, however, overestimates Paul D's empathy for her struggle. He is sorrowful for those indignities of Sethe's experience which his own suffering corroborates. But, perhaps as a man, he cannot fully accept the maternal weight of her breasts. He had first "held them as though they were the most expensive part of himself," (21) so eager is he to absorb Sethe's pain, but after their first lovemaking (as if to foreshadow his abandonment), Paul D is repulsed by Sethe's breasts. In these moments he symbolically rejects Sethe's protean identity as woman and mother. He cannot understand a "used-to-be-slave woman['s]" love for her children, and he fears Sethe's declaration to protect her daughter "while I'm live and . . . when I ain't" (45). Paul D has no context for Sethe's independence or her "thick" love (164); he is incapable of measuring its heft and, in his own helplessness, feebly reminds her that she has "two feet . . . not four" (165), intimating that only a beast could kill its young. His words are harsher than his intent, but once they are spoken, "a forest sprang up between them" (165). Sethe will not tolerate any reduction of her selfhood (from Schoolteacher's listing her parts or Paul D's counting her feet). She rebuffs all attempts to minimize her victories as a woman, as a mother. And so she takes back from Paul D the responsibility for her breasts that she had given a short time earlier.

Sethe never questions her womanhood as Paul D does his manhood. He has endured the sadism of slaveholding and survived its hellish aftermath; yet, he cannot commit himself to Sethe and share her sorrow. He has taken his own advice to Sethe and learned not to love too much, because if one loved too much, one or the object of that love may be destroyed. Paul D wonders, then, if he is the man he always thought himself to be. At Sweet Home, Garner had encouraged his defiance, independence, and decision making. He and the others had been allowed to "buy a mother, choose a horse or a wife, handle guns, even learn reading if they wanted to" (125). But these privileges of humanity were only available at Sweet Home and only under Garner. "One step off that ground and they were trespassers among the human race" (125). The day Schoolteacher puts a bit in his mouth for trying to escape is the day Paul D comes to terms with these certainties. He tells Sethe that on that day, as the last of the Sweet Home men, "wasn't no way I'd ever be Paul D again, living or dead. Schoolteacher changed me" (72). In order to continue with his life, Paul D had replaced his "red heart" with a "tobacco tin buried in his chest. . . . Its lid rusted shut" (72–73). In that condition he comes to Sethe but cannot remain. Sethe's heart, on the other hand, is conditioned by motherlove. She does not doubt its function. Children are incarnate proof of her woman's identity.

Morrison's implicit contrast of Sethe and Paul D is not a faultfinding mission against Paul D or against men in general but rather is a delineation of Sethe's character. She uses Paul D in much the same way she does the community: to set Sethe's extraordinary strength in relief. Conflict becomes a strategy. Like the community, Paul D eventually returns to Sethe's rescue. When she sinks under the burden of responsibility she had borne alone for so long, Paul D is there to offer relief once more, but this time he does not waiver. Once before he had embraced her life with the force of masculine intent and desire: arousing Sethe's sexual passion; criticizing her daughter, Denver; evicting the baby ghost; proscribing Sethe's responses. This time, however, his presence is conditioned by feminine principles of compassion, nurturance, and patience. He offers to bathe Sethe, including her "exhausted breasts" (172), Sethe hopes. This time Sethe can tell him things that women "only tell each other." She can transcend the bounds of her rebellion against Schoolteacher (which informs the bravado of her first explanation to Paul D of what happened in the woodshed) and cry for the absent sons and her dead daughter, who was her "best thing" (272). This time Paul D does not judge Sethe or feel betrayed by her stamina: "He wants to put his story *next* to hers" (273; emphasis added). This time he does not count her feet but reminds her that she is her "best thing." He can accept her yesterdays and share her tomorrows.

Despite his early retreat from deep feeling, Paul D is a nurturer at his core. He is "the kind of man who can walk in a house and make the women cry. Because with him, in his presence, they could" (272). But like other men in Morrison's work, he has the spirit of a wanderer. He is another of Morrison's traveling men who resist domesticity. He is compulsively mobile "because he didn't believe he could live with a woman—any woman—for over two out of three months. That was about as long as he could abide one place" (40). Slavery has birthed a fear of place that is quieted only when he is moving. Like Cholly and Ajax he is conditioned by oppressive circumstances to crave freedom. Paul D is different from them, however. He is not dangerously free like Cholly (who, when he is overcome by pity for his daughter's pathetic helplessness, rapes her), nor is he as self-absorbed as Ajax (who loves but one woman—his mother). Paul D's wanderlust spawns less-debilitating character defects and ends at 124 when his compassion for Sethe quells his fear of being entrapped.

Paul D's presence in *Beloved* serves Morrison's second literary goal (the first is delineating Sethe's identity as a strong woman who so much loved something other than herself): to portray the lives of slaves in a way that has not been done before. As a black woman and student of American history (both the canonized and revised versions), Morrison is familiar with slaves' lives as those lives are presented in memoir.[11] These narratives recount the cruelty and inhumanity of slavery. Morrison notes, however, that in their efforts to be objective, to not "offend the reader by being too angry, or by showing two much outrage, or by calling the reader names,"[12] slave narrators pulled the veil over "proceedings too terrible to relate." Morrison aims to remove that veil and recreate "the interior life" that was deliberately excised "from the records that the slaves themselves told."[13] The reader should not merely *know* about the horror of slavery but *feel* what it was like. The extent to which she does this is the extent to which she writes beyond the record of slavery. The published account of Margaret Garner's crime is totally subordinate to the unpublished interior life, just as the published recollections of male narrators do not go as far as Paul D's truth; Morrison fills in and updates.

Unlike the narrators Morrison is under no constraint to please her audience. Neither is she constrained by the narrators' need for verity, to keep facts straight. She has artistic freedom. In one view, then, the difference between slave autobiography and *Beloved* is the difference between autobiography and fiction. In effect, *Beloved* is directed by the creative process which holds all good writers in tow by engaging the author's imagination and demanding attention to her characters' interior lives. But Morrison's relationship to her subject and characters is not entirely explained by the art of fiction. She does acknowledge that her work is imaginative, but more important, it is also truthful. Truthful does not mean recounting verifiable details of specific events, places, and people as in the approach which Morrison calls the "oh, yes, this is where he or she got it from school."[14] It does mean absolute fidelity to the subject. In *Beloved* it means fidelity to the slaves' experiences. The truth of slavery is its contamination of humanity, its agency of evil, and that truth lies beyond the specific details of suffering of any individual. Truth transcends time, place, and audience, and it gives universal insight. It is more spiritual than intellectual. It is the difference between Margaret Garner's personal truth and humanity's impersonal truth. Morrison arrives at this truth through her own memory—not particular memories of slavery, of course—but a personal (and seemingly unrelated) memory that gives her almost clairvoyant access to the interior lives of characters. For Morrison, then, writing Paul D, Sethe, and the community of *Beloved* was more than a mental exercise acted upon by the imagination to turn thoughts into art. It was, through inclusion of her memories, an act of writing a part of herself into the narrative. The result is a view of slavery not undertaken before. As she says, "they [her characters] are my entrance into my own interior life."[15]

While *Beloved* was in progress, for example, Morrison had a recurring image of corn on the cob which evoked converging memories of her early life: the house where she grew up in Lorain, Ohio; her parents' working in the garden; eating hot and cold corn in the summer in the midst of extended family and neighbors who stopped in. The corn is sweet finger food Morrison remembers.[16] "The picture of the corn," she says, "and the nimbus of emotion surrounding it became a powerful one" in *Beloved*.[17] Morrison does not say what scenes that emotion prompted, but perhaps the sweet corn of her childhood became the succulent blackberries picked by Stamp Paid, and perhaps the "easy" mood of her summers in Ohio became the satisfying fulfillment of those invited to Baby Suggs's community party to eat berry pies. The mood of that moment of celebration (which begins with a bucket of blackberries and explodes into a feast of pies, pan-fried perch, rabbit, corn pudding, chicken, and watermelon punch) stands out in its stark contrast to other moods in the novel. During an afternoon and evening ninety former slaves please and indulge themselves with an uncommon abandon. Then celebration turns to vexation, to envy, and finally to malicious withdrawal. Those who had enjoyed Baby Suggs's generosity were suddenly too resentful to warn her of the coming danger. In her signature style Morrison portrays the contradictory emotions that drive human behavior: ninety people eat so well and laugh so much they become not joyful but angry; simultaneously, they savor Baby Suggs's liberality, and they punish what they believe is the arrogance that begets it, with their own arrogance.

That scene takes less than two pages to tell, but its brevity belies its strategic importance. It becomes the radiating "nimbus" of Sethe's conflict with the community and of Baby Suggs's defeat. And it subtly but distinctly colors the murder, heightening the sorrow. The knowledge of betrayal by the community haunts the scene and challenges readers' credulity: how, the reader asks, could people have behaved so? Schoolteacher's pursuit of Sethe and her children is no surprise, but her own people's withdrawal reverberates throughout the text. The story strains toward an explanation and resolution. Not surprisingly, Morrison offers no explanation. She understands the authority of ambiguity in the human experience. Resolution comes many years later in the final pages, when the community of women prevent Sethe from committing another murder. Weakened and disoriented from her ordeal with the incubus, Beloved, Sethe sees Edward Bodwin drive into her yard and imagines that Schoolteacher has returned for her best thing. She turns upon the unsuspecting Bodwin with an ice pick, but before he is even aware of any danger, the women knock Sethe to the ground. This time they salvage Sethe from death and murder and in so doing return to their natural function as a refuge and reservoir of knowledge for the individual. They understand, even if Sethe does not, the power of the incubus, and they do not fear it. Their own collective will is greater. At last they gather before Sethe's house, not in recalcitrant silence, but with raised voices, searching "for the right combination, the key, the code, the sound that broke the back of words. Building voice upon voice until they found it and when they did, it was a wave of sound wide enough to sound deep water and knock pods off chestnut trees. It broke over Sethe and she trembled like the baptized in its wash" (261). Sethe is reborn in a primordial ceremony of engulfing sound. For her the women's "loving faces" (262) recall the twenty-eight days of fellowship she had once known in their midst. It is as if Baby Suggs's ministry of love has finally come to fruition and is nourishment for Sethe.

Unveiling these interior lives of her characters carries with it titanic responsibility for Morrison. She is continuing an unfinished script of slavery begun over two centuries ago by the first slave narrative, and she must do it truthfully and with integrity. Morrison's characters stand in for all those slaves and former slaves who were "unceremoniously buried" without tribute or recognition. She feels chosen by them to attend to their burial "properly, artistically."[18] Beloved is her effort to do that. It is an act of recovering the past in narrative, to "insert this memory that was unbearable and unspeakable into the literature."[19] Only then is it possible, Morrison believes, for black people, for society, to move on. This need to remember before moving on is reflected in the epilogue, where, after having passed on Beloved's story, Morrison writes in contradiction that "this is not a story to pass on" (275). It threatens peace of mind and must be resisted. To protect themselves, the community forgot Beloved: "Disremembered and unaccounted for, she cannot be lost because no one is looking for her, and even if they were, how can they call her if they don't know her name? Although she has claim, she is not claimed" (274). This is not a story to pass on, and yet Morrison acknowledges that ironically "it is not a story to pass by."[20] Only by remembering the past can there be liberation from its burden.

Although the setting and scope of Beloved is primarily slavery in the American South, Morrison wants to recover all facets of the slave's story—from Africa to America. Brief images of Sethe in a place where she "take[s] flowers away from leaves [and] . . . puts them in a round basket" (210) suggest an Africa of beauty and freedom before white violence and enslavement.[21] Morrison also captures the heartbreak of the middle passage, the slave route from Africa to the West Indies, during which many perished in cargo holds or jumped from ships to death in the sea. This, Morrison thinks, is the least examined aspect of slavery. "No one praised them, nobody knows their names, nobody can remember them, not in the United States nor in Africa. Millions of people disappeared without a trace, and there is not one monument anywhere to pay homage to them, because they never arrived safely on shore. So it's like a whole nation that is under the sea."[22] Beloved inhabits this place under blue water before she is reincarnated at 124, and as Karla Holloway notes, she is "not only Sethe's dead daughter returned, but the return[ed] of all the faces, all the drowned, but remembered, faces of mothers and their children who have lost their being because of the force of that EuroAmerican slave-history."[23]

Writing *Beloved* required a modicum of emotional risk for Morrison. Recovering truth was sometimes "very intense," she says. She would "write a sentence and . . . jump up and run outside or something." This kind of story "sort of beats you up."[24] But during the difficult times she reminded herself: "All I have to do is to think about the people who lived there, who lived through it. If they could live it, I could write about it."[25] That is the way Morrison works—with an intensity and focus that can be isolating: "There is a temptation to draw away from living people, people who are extremely important to you and who are real. They're in competition a great deal with this collection of imagined characters."[26] Morrison converses with her characters, literally speaks aloud to them; they become a collection of "graphic presences." She acknowledges that this is not "the vocabulary of literary criticism," but it is, she claims, the way any writer whose work she respects speaks about her work. And it is often the vocabulary of black women writers.[27]

"The work that I do," Morrison says, "frequently falls in the minds of most people, into that realm of fiction called fantastic, or mythic, or magical, or unbelievable."[28] She is "not comfortable with these labels" because they suggest a breech with truth, and her "single gravest responsibility (in spite of that magic) is not to lie."[29] Morrison names this aspect of her work "enchantment" and says she uses it "simply because that's the way the world was for me and for the black people that I knew. In addition to the very shred, down-to-earth, efficient way in which they did things and survived things, there was this other knowledge or perception, always discredited but nevertheless there, which informed their sensibilities and clarified their activities."[30] Beloved gives a context to these comments. It has been pointed to as an example of Morrison's magical real style. Indeed, a toddling infant who is reincarnated as a young woman with new skin, rudimentary language, breath like new milk, and the cravings and temper of a child is fantastic; but it is also artistically credible. It validates Sethe's claims that she is a tough mother who will protect her children in life and in death. She sent her daughter not to death and nothingness, but to another life from which she returns "of her own free will" (200). This scenario saves the novel from becoming a melodramatic tale of murder and pathos (although one could not imagine Morrison authoring such stuff).[31] Sethe transcends the limitations placed upon her in slavery and becomes the agent of her own fate. In this plot Sethe is not subject to any authority outside herself—not Schoolteacher's, Paul D's, Stamp Paid's, or anyone else's in the community. By the same token she is also not subject to any conventional punishment. She may be jailed and ostracized, but she remains stead-fast in the rightness of her action until Beloved's return. Only then does she weaken, in the presence of the only one capable of tormenting her, "the one and only person she felt she had to convince, that what she had done was right because it came from true love" (251).

Of course Beloved, though she is twenty-one, is temperamentally the child whose emotional growth was arrested in the woodshed. She is selfish, demanding, greedy for Sethe's love, her attention, her self. Her demands drain Sethe to the point that "Beloved . . . looked the mother, Sethe the . . . child . . . confined to a corner," (250) muttering feebly to an implacable ghost. Ironically, the very love that earlier gives Sethe the strength to save herself for her children betrays her into a sacrifice of self. And it is a different sacrifice from going to the gallows for killing her children to "save them." This sacrifice is not born of conviction, but of guilt and fear. This sacrifice erodes her identity. By the time the thirty neighborhood women appear in her yard, Sethe has "yielded up her life [to Beloved] without a murmur" (250). Beloved's return, then, gives Morrison an opportunity to explore the circumference of Sethe's character. Endurance joins halting fear. As resilient as she is, she is also vulnerable, and her strength and weak-ness emanate from the same stream of love. "It's peculiar to women," Morrison believes, that "the best thing . . . in us is also the thing that makes us sabotage ourselves."[32]

The love that gives Sethe courage in the woodshed and bitter triumph over Schoolteacher and slavery makes her vulnerable to the manipulations of a ghost child. She had been willing to die with and for that child to keep her from slavery; years later, she willingly enslaves herself to the incubus whom she continues to believe is her best thing. The love that sustained her threatens to consume her. Perhaps this is retribution; even righteous crimes such as Sethe's have a reckoning. But Sethe's journey does not end there. When the novel closes, she is on the verge of new understanding. Her children are free, and finally it is possible for Sethe to learn that, as Paul D tells her, she is her best thing.

Notes

1. Gloria Naylor and Toni Morrison: "A Conversation," *Southern Review* 21 (1985): 588. Morrison says that she was compelled to do what she thought others had not because she was "ill-taught"; she did not know the work of black women writers like Zora Neale Hurston or Paule Marshall.

2. Naylor and Morrison 588.

3. Naylor and Morrison 583.

4. Naylor and Morrison 583–84.

5. Naylor and Morrison 585.

6. Toni Morrison, *Beloved* (New York: Alfred A. Knopf, 1987) 163. Subsequent references will appear in parentheses in the text.

7. Naylor and Morrison 584.

8. Angels Carabi, "Toni Morrison," *Belles Lettres* (Winter 1994): 89.

9. Morrison is expressing the African principle of death as transition and liberation. According to this eschatology "death is not a destruction of the individual. Life goes on beyond the grave," a view that effectively undermines the slaveholder's power over his slave by dissolving the fear of death. See John S. Mibiti, *African Religions and Philosophy* (Garden City, N. Y.: Doubleday, 1970) 113.

10. Alice Walker's womanist theory, which is concerned with the survival of an entire people, male and female, seems appropriate here. See Alice Walker, *In Search of Our Mothers' Gardens* (San Diego: Harcourt Brace, 1984).

11. Narratives of slaves' experiences in slavery and in freedom flourished before and after the Civil War. For an examination of slave narrative and the African-American literary tradition, see Deborah E. McDowell and Arnold Rampersad, eds., *Slavery and the Literary Imagination* (Baltimore: Johns Hopkins University Press, 1989); William Andrews, *To Tell a Free Story: The First Century of Afro-American Autobiography, 1760–1865;* and others.

12. Toni Morrison, "The Site of Memory," *Inventing the Truth: The Art and Craft of Memoir,* ed. William Zinsser (Boston: Houghton Mifflin, 1987) 106.

13. Morrison, "Site" 110–11.

14. Morrison, "Site" 112.

15. Morrison, "Site" 115.

16. Morrison, "Site" 118.

17. Morrison, "Site" 118.

18. Naylor and Morrison 585.

19. Carabi 88.

20. Carabi 88.

21. Morrison acknowledges that "it may be a little too romantic to think about Africa as a kind of Eden, before corruption, the cradle of humanity." With Sethe's image she intended to communicate "a picture of community" that was unconquered. See Carabi 86.

22. Carabi 88.

23. Karla F. C. Holloway, "*Beloved:* A Spiritual," *Callaloo* 13 (1990): 522.

24. Morrison, "Site" 122.

25. Carabi 90.

26. Naylor and Morrison 586.

27. Naylor and Morrison 586.

28. Morrison, "Site" 112.

29. Morrison, "Site" 112–13.

30. Christina Davis, "Interview with Toni Morrison," *Presence Africaine* (First Quarterly 1988). Rpt. in *Toni Morrison: Critical Perspectives Past and Present,* ed. Henry Louis Gates, Jr., and K. A. Appiah (New York: Amistad, 1993) 414.

31. The exception to this critical view of Morrison's achievement is Stanley Crouch's review of *Beloved* in which he asserts that Morrison stereotypes and simplifies complex human motivations. See Stanley Crouch, "Review of *Beloved,* by Toni Morrison," *New Republic* 19 (October 1987): 38–43.

32. Naylor and Morrison 585.

6

CITY BLUES

JAZZ

Five years after the publication of *Beloved,* Morrison returned to the image of the dead girl in Van der Zee's photograph collection, *The Harlem Book of the Dead.* In *Jazz* (1992) eighteen-year-old Dorcas Manfred embodies Morrison's curiosity about a young dying woman who sacrifices herself to save her lover by refusing to name him as her murderer.

Morrison's original interest in the story related to a broader fascination with women's unselfishness—the willingness by some to value people they love more than themselves. By the time she wrote *Jazz,* however, Morrison's focus had changed. (She had, after all, just finished writing about Sethe, a woman who loves too much, in *Beloved.*) Dorcas is neither noble nor selfless. She is shallow and manipulative. When shot by her married lover, she bleeds to death because she will not seek medical help. Any magnanimity intended by shielding her boyfriend's identity is spoiled by a foolish insistence upon waiting until morning for treatment. She apparently fears discovery of her transgressions more than she does death.

Dorcas, then, is not a sympathetic character whose life and death, if they were given the exemplary Morrison treatment, have the potential to both inspire and disgust. That role goes to fifty-four-year-old Joe Trace, a married man who loves his wife, seduces and falls in love with an eighteen-year-old girl, and then shoots her when she leaves him. Joe shares the role with his wife, Violet, who crashes Dorcas's funeral to attack a girl who is already dead. Dorcas's death and funeral center the story and characters, serving as a recurring point of return and reference, but once the crime is named, typically, Morrison moves to a review of the criminals. Crime and punishment do not concern Morrison, but people and motivation do.[1] What kind of man desires a girl young enough to be his daughter, even his granddaughter? Why does he harm her? What kind of woman walks into a funeral in progress and assaults a dead body with a knife? If they are not psychopaths (and they never are in Morrison's work), then they are merely interesting people and extraordinary specimens of the human condition: they are good people who do bad things. "The combination of virtue and flaw, of good intentions gone awry, of wickedness cleansed and people made whole again," interests Morrison. She does not judge characters by "the worst that they have done" or by the best, but the "combinations . . . are the best part of writing novels."[2]

Joe and Violet are two lonely people whose love for each other cannot penetrate dense walls of disappointment and pain. When he can no longer turn to his wife for companionship and intimacy, Joe looks for someone else and finds Dorcas. In a way Violet also finds her. After the shooting Violet obtains a photograph of the girl and places it on the living room mantle, where she and Joe take turns alternately admiring it and being moved to tears by it. For each the picture is a reminder of lost opportunities for living and loving: Dorcas is the mother Joe was never able to love and protect, and she is the daughter Violet never bore. In a peculiar way Dorcas's death is the bridge that links their paths back to each other. Sorrow bonds them, and ultimately they are reconciled with their losses and renewed in life and love.

Morrison does not brand Joe Trace as an immoral man. He and Violet are good people whose circumstances shape their bizarre behavior. Shooting Dorcas is the exception in his otherwise blemishless life. Before and after, Joe is

A nice neighborly, everybody-knows-him man. The kind you let in your house because he was not dangerous, because you had seen him with children, bought his products and never heard a scrap of gossip about him doing wrong. Felt not only safe but kindly in his company because he was the sort women ran to when they thought they were being followed, or watched or needed someone to have the extra key just in case you locked yourself out. He was the man who took you to your door if you missed the trolley and had to walk night streets at night. Who warned young girls away from hooch joints and the men who lingered there. Women teased him because they trusted him.[3]

For the most part Joe lives up to this summary assessment of his character. With Dorcas he is paternal, kind—not exactly in the way of a doting, indulgent father, but more like a wise, generous lover. He brings her gifts, confesses his deepest doubts and fears, and perhaps as the best evidence of his love, accepts her as she is. With Violet he is also touchingly affectionate. By the time Joe finds Dorcas, his marriage is routine, lonely and silent—Violet speaks only to her birds; there is no intimacy. Joe cannot even remember the way their lives used to be when they were young and in love. He recalls events, "but he has a tough time trying to catch what it felt like" (29). Despite Violet's distance, however, Joe continues to care about her. He may have lost the energy of his love, but the affection remains. His passion for Dorcas does not threaten that affection. He would never intentionally hurt Violet.

And he does not *intentionally* or with deliberation hurt Dorcas. Morrison does not provide explicit reasons for Joe's violence, and yet the emotions which propel him toward Dorcas on the night of the shooting are entirely comprehensible. They are not the ordinary passions of violence: rage, fury, malice, anger. In fact, on that evening he feels and thinks very little. The hunter that he was in youth emerges, and he follows Dorcas's trail instinctively, doggedly, across New York's boroughs. In the beauty parlor women speculate about a man Joe's age asking questions with embarrassing urgency about a girl barely out of high school. A neighbor looks with a knowing and disapproving smile at his foolish demeanor. The search is pathetic, hopeless, sorrowful. For five days he traces her movements, reviews her scheduled appointments, analyzes the discrepancies. Finally, he tracks her to a crowded apartment where she is locked in a dancing embrace with a new, younger lover, swaying back and forth to the steamy music. At that moment Joe's "rambling . . . rambling all through the City" (130) is over. He has the gun but he believes it is the hand with which he wants to touch her. When he heard "the gun go thuh!" he wanted to "catch her before she fell and hurt herself" (130).

The tempest is hardly discernable. Joe loves Dorcas before, and he loves her after—and most likely he loves her at the instant he aims the gun and pulls the trigger. Unable or unwilling to leave her, as Dorcas had urged him to do, Joe tracks her to "help" her clarify their need for each other, to help her realize that he is "a mild man" (183) who "know[s] how to treat a woman," who "never would mistreat one. Never would make a woman live like a dog in a cave" (182). He needs her acknowledgement that he belongs to her. But like Joe's mother—the naked woman who lived wild in the caves and woods of Virginia while he was growing up—Dorcas abandons him, does not claim him. In searching for one Joe also searches for the other. The trail across the streets of New York becomes, in Joe's mind, the viney, treacherous Virginia woods where he hunted the woman who was said to be his mother, in order to be granted a glimmer of recognition. Joe never finds his mother. After the third abortive search his hurt feelings compete with feelings of anger and humiliation that his mother would choose a cave and not him. He does, however, find Dorcas. But she too has chosen not to give or receive his love. Perhaps shooting Dorcas discharges the pent-up misery and humiliation of his past.

Any convenient psychoanalytical view of Joe's repressed intentions (no matter how much such a view is supported by the text) should not obscure Morrison's characterization of him as a kind man and, more important, as a sane one. Before the day he sets out to locate Dorcas with a gun in his pocket, he is level-headed, prudent, discreet, reasonable. Those essential ingredients of his character do not change in the course of the narrative; they are only temporarily arrested. Morrison suggests, as she always does of deranged episodes in otherwise rational lives, that no definitive, easy-to-grasp explanation exists for the exception. Some experiences are paradoxical and irreconcilable. As Morrison's mysterious narrator observes in *Jazz*, "trying to figure out anybody's state of mind" (137) is risky.

For that reason perhaps (and also because Joe is not directly responsible for Dorcas's death; she could have saved herself by getting medical help), Morrison does not send Joe off to prison for his crime. Obviously, banishment would not serve Morrison's structure, which situates her characters within a community nor would it serve her perennial interest in the individual's relationship to that community. Instead, she gives Joe an opportunity for redemption. In self-imposed detention in his apartment, Joe spends his days crying and his nights staring at the photograph of Dorcas that sits on the mantlepiece. Through heartfelt anguish and grief Joe discovers forgiveness and peace of mind. His punishment is the knowledge that even if he "didn't kill her outright; even if she made herself die" (212), he is to blame. As he says, "It was me. For the rest of my life, it'll be me" (212). But, as he stares into Dorcas's picture, he sees in her face no regret, no accusation: "No finger points. Her lips don't turn down in judgement" (12). In time Joe accepts this dichotomy of guilt and innocence and moves forward with life.

Joe is the most recent variation on Morrison's prototypical male. At the core this kind of man likes women. Even the most embryonic, emotionally unevolved male protagonist in Morrison's fiction has at least a kernel of this unlibidinous affection for women. In Joe this quality achieves maturity. After observing him, Dorcas's young friend, Felice, innocently compares him to other men she has known and to her father. Joe is the domestic sort who trims his wife's hair, whose generosity and warmth are reflected in his eyes, which allow an observer to "look inside him" and which look "inside you" (206). When Joe looks at Felice, she feels "deep" as if her feelings and thoughts "are important and different and . . . interesting" (206). She concludes that Joe "likes women" without "flirt[ing] with them" and that contrary to prevailing community sentiments, Joe especially "likes his wife" (206).

Violet, Joe's wife, is a study in madness, the type of contained craziness that suggests a strenuous but unsuccessful effort to keep one's life in balance. In consequence, the fabric of Violet's once cohesive, conventional existence persistently unravels into loose threads of lunacy. Attacking Dorcas in her coffin is one of several frayed edges. Helpless to stop herself, Violet watches as a woman she recognizes but does not know elbows her way through the mourners in a crowded church, stops at the coffin with her knife raised, and, before she is wrestled to the floor by ushers, manages to nick the dead girl's neck. Another time she had stopped on her way to an appointment and sat in the street. "She didn't stumble nor was she pushed: she just sat down" (17). Violet is also tormented by "a renegade tongue yearning to be on its own" (21). Sometimes she has no control over it, and she hears speech that is without context or rational meaning. Fearful of these times, Violet retreats into silence, relying upon "'Oh' or 'have mercy' [to] carry almost all of her part of a conversation" (24). Over time she only feels safe speaking to the caged parrot in her apartment.

Violet had not always been pathetic. Her days had not always been punctuated by public and private craziness. As a girl and young woman in Virginia, she had hauled hay, broken cane, chopped wood. As a married woman in New York,

She had been a snappy, determined girl and a hardworking young woman, with the snatch-gossip tongue of a beautician. She liked, and had, to get her way. . . . She had butted their way out of the Tenderloin district into a spacious uptown apartment promised to another family by sitting out the landlord, haunting his doorway. She collected customers by going up to them and describing her services ("I can do your hair better and cheaper, and do it when and where you want"). She argued butchers and wagon vendors into prime and extra ("Put that little end piece in. You weighing the stalks; I'm buying the leaf"). (23)

But by the time she is fifty, Violet is transformed from nervy ambition to cracked silence.

Morrison renders Violet's lapses from normalcy without judgement as though emotional exigency is just another aspect of the human predicament, as though huge allowance must be made for the variances of conduct. Once such allowance is made, no eyebrow need be raised in condemnation. On the contrary, Morrison exhibits a regard for Violet and confers on her the madwoman's insight. For example, Violet rightly observes, without malice, that Dorcas "was ugly. Outside and in" (205). She visits Alice Manfred, Dorcas's aunt, not to apologize—for anything—but rather innocently to find answers "to see what kind of girl" Joe would choose over her (82). Indeed, between Alice and Violet, "No apology or courtesy seemed required or necessary. . . . But something else was—clarity. . . . The kind of clarity crazy people demand from the not crazy" (83). Because Violet has lost so much—peace of mind, focus, direction—she has little to fear from hearing and speaking truth. With Violet the always proper Alice can forgo the facade of social convention. She can be "impolite. Sudden. Frugal" (83), but mostly she can be honest. With Violet, Alice is forced to see not only her niece's lie with Joe, but her own deceptions. She can no longer set herself apart, pretend to be different from other women—common women, who are enraged and deranged by a husband's betrayal. In the face of Violet's assertion that Dorcas is her enemy even in death and that is why she attacked her, Alice suddenly, reluctantly remembers repressed images of violence against the other woman in her own married life. Thirty years earlier, she had craved not her husband's blood but death and torment to the woman he had chosen instead of her. Alice had not acted but had contented herself with murderous dreams. And because she had been restrained then, now Alice is fearful of women like Violet who are not—until she gets to know Violet and comes nose to nose with their similarity to each other.

In some ways Violet's life is Morrison's window for viewing the lives of all black women who have been wronged. Morrison calls them "armed" and "dangerous" (77) because many carry "folded blades, packets of lye,

shards of glass taped to their hands" (78). Those who do not arm themselves are "attached to armed men" (78). Still others "become pistols"
organizing "leagues, clubs, societies, sisterhoods . . . [designed to] bail
out, dress the dead, pay the rent, find new rooms, start a school, storm an
office, take up collections, rent the block and keep their eyes on all the
children" (78). These are the resolute women who are united in struggle.
Whether they struggle to keep a man, whether the fight is for room and
board or for personal dignity, is unimportant. For Morrison they detail a
single composite pattern.

That is the point Morrison makes with Alice and Violet's relationship.
Despite their differences—Alice is one of the "pistols" organizing chari-
table women's clubs; Violet is one of the armed; Alice's niece is shot by
Violet's husband—they find unlikely comfort and friendship with each other.
Alice is prepared, when Violet first comes to see her, to look down from a
mountaintop of superiority and propriety. But Violet will allow no such
unexamined response: "We women, me and you. Tell me something real.
. . . I'm fifty and I don't know nothing" (110). She means do not judge me
or dismiss me; look at your life and tell me what lessons, if any, you have
learned in fifty-seven years that can help make my life intelligible. To such
frankness and vulnerability, Alice can only moan, "Oh Mama" (110). And
Violet does the same. In that moment they are linked by mutual compassion, to each other and also to ancestral women. In that moment they
occupy a space in the line formed by generations of struggling black women.

Perhaps Alice is remembering some particular aspect of her mother
when she responds to Violet. Certainly, Violet is remembering her mother,
who had fought for life and lost. Rose Dear had scratched out a living in
Virginia after her husband left. But with five children and no help, she did
not last long. When the sheriff came and took everything, including the
chair Rose was sitting in, she was defeated. Four years later she jumped to
her death down a well shaft. Violet recalls her mother's desperation in the
wake of her own, and the recollection prompts her to ask: "Mama? Is this
where you got to and couldn't do it no more?" (110). Was there one final
assault that pushed you beyond the edge of endurance and made suicide
the best choice?

Violet does not contemplate suicide, but she is nevertheless facing a
crossroads of decision: should she leave Joe or should she take another
lover? (After Dorcas's death she had halfheartedly taken one whose name
she cannot remember.) Should she fall back in love with Joe and try to

repair her broken life with him? Violet puts these questions to Alice, who advises her to "mind what's left to you" (113) because "little bitty life" is too "small and quick" (113) to do anything less. Alice has learned this the hard way. Not until it is too late does she realize that with her niece she had substituted policing for nurturing. She had tried in vain to forestall Dorcas's maturing into a woman because she feared the youthful passions that might claim Dorcas and transform her into one of the other women. Ironically, her fears are realized in Dorcas's fatal rebellion. Alice warns Violet not to allow her fears about the future with Joe to boomerang. As if to underscore her point, Alice unintentionally burns a blouse that she is pressing when she leaves the iron on the fabric too long. The scorched spot is like a painful episode in a life. At first the women stare at the ruined material in shocked disbelief, and then they disintegrate into healing laughter. "Crumpled over, shoulders shaking, Violet thought about how she must have looked at the funeral, at what her mission was. The sight of herself trying to do something bluesy, something hep, fumbling the knife, too late anyway. . . . She laughed till she coughed and Alice had to make them both a cup of settling tea" (114).

Violet and Joe fix what is wrong in their lives and continue on together. Like those of many other Morrison characters, their crimes are redeemed by suffering and by spiritual enlightenment. Joe comes to understand that although he had been *in* love twice, he "didn't know *how* to love anybody" (213; emphasis added). He would not squander a third opportunity. Violet realizes that sleeping with a doll to satisfy the hunger for a baby and permitting herself other acts of lunacy have a high price. When she awakens from self-induced oblivion, "her husband had shot a girl young enough to be that daughter" (109) she hungers for. In the future she will "mind" what is left to her. Joe and Violet find love again—not the first love of passion and desire or the follow-up love of anguish and regrets—but a kind that is tranquil and deeply satisfying, a love of long walks, good meals, afternoon naps in each other's arms. "A lot of the time . . . they stay home figuring things out, telling each other those little personal stories they like to hear again and again . . ." (223).

Morrison's novels are said to be about place and displacement, referring to her communities, which are strongly evocative of mood, culture, psychology, and to her characters, who are often alienated from the people and places that give them identity. In these ways *Jazz* is typical of Morrison's work: the place is New York City, and Morrison's characters are both seduced and repulsed by it. Joe and Violet moved to New York from the

South like many others between the turn of the century and World War I. And like these others they were motivated to move by political and economic hard times in the South and by the hope of better times in the North. For the most part their hopes were realized. At first Violet found domestic work until she settled on doing hair, and Joe "worked everything from whitefolks shoe leather" to cleaning fish and toilets before finding better work conditions and better pay as a full-time hotel waiter who sold lady's cosmetics on the side. They moved four times in about seven years, the fourth time to Lenox Avenue in a Harlem that is now just a memory. "The buildings were like castles in pictures" (127) with five- , six- , and ten-room apartments. Joe and Violet "had birds and plants everywhere," and they "made sure the front was as neat as the inside" (127). The city offered them possibility, the chance to remake themselves in the images of their dreams which had been fueled in part by long-distance reports of Baltimore from those who had gone there and believed they had found a new promised land:

> The money to be earned for doing light work—standing in front of a door, carrying food on a tray, even cleaning strangers' shoes—got you in a day more money than any of them had earned in one whole harvest. White people literally threw money at you—just for being neighborly: opening a taxi door, picking up a package. And anything you had or made or found you could sell in the streets. In fact, there were streets where colored people owned all the stores; whole blocks of handsome colored men and women laughing all night and making money all day. Steel cars sped down the streets and if you saved up, they said, you could get you one and drive as long as there was road. (106)

For Joe and Violet the dream place was New York and not Baltimore, but it too was wonderful. In 1906 they boarded a northbound train. As they approached the city, it "was speaking to them. . . . And like a million others, chests pointing, tracks controlling their feet, they stared out the windows for first sight of the City that danced with them, proving already how much it loved them" (32). When they "danced on into the City . . . they knew right away that perfect was not the word. It [New York] was better than that," (107) especially for a couple who had no children and did not want any—"citylife would be so much better without them" (107). Being on Lenox Avenue was "worth anything" because it marked the boundary of a pulsing black world of economic progress.

Sometime, however, during twenty years of keeping the beat of city rhythms, Joe and Violet lose their way. Violet is first, and then Joe. The city deludes Violet into thinking she can be who she is not: "White. Light. Young again" (208). These are childhood longings nurtured by her grandmother's stories of the little blond Golden Gray, the child of Miss Vera Louise and a slave boy on her father's plantation. True Belle, a slave herself, had taken care of Vera Louise and later her golden-haired son in Baltimore, where the three of them had gone when the daughter was no longer welcome at the plantation. In going to Baltimore, True Belle left behind a sister, a husband, and two daughters, ages eight and ten. Twenty-two years later when one daughter, Rose Dear, gave up on life, True Belle returned with ten dollars, "Baltimore tales for granddaughters," and descriptions of life with the wonderful Golden Gray: "How they bathed him three times a day, and how the G on he underwear was embroidered with blue thread. The shape of the tub and what they put in the water to make him smell like honeysuckle sometimes and sometimes of lavender" (142). In Violet's little girl imagination, Golden Gray was sometimes transformed into a young girl, always living inside her "mind. Quiet as a mole" (207), dormant until in New York old stories of city glamour, golden beauty, and privilege surfaced and began to shape her needs. By the time she realizes the deception, her life is already "messed up" (208). She is a lonely, silent woman craving the child (a daughter, she thinks) she once aborted. Before she "came North . . . [Violet] made sense and so did the world. . . . [She] didn't have nothing but . . . [she] didn't miss it" (207). At fifty, in the city, she and her world are incoherent. "Twenty years in a city better than perfect" (111) is not what Violet thought it would be.

Joe is correspondingly desolate. Living an empty routine with a woman who carries a doll to bed and talks only to a parrot leaves Joe feeling more alone that he ever did in "his fields and woods and secret lonely valleys" of Virginia (107). This simple need for belonging that makes Joe the neighborly, trustworthy man that he is and that the city cannot obliterate finds distorted expression in Joe's relationship to Dorcas. With her he is no longer lonely, but paradoxically, with her he also violates himself. He becomes the kind of man who "*knew* wrong wasn't right, and did it anyway" (74). Joe had gone to New York in search of his new self, his better self, but the quest is derailed. In Tyrell, Virginia, he had been a sharecropper. In New York he expected to find dignity and spirit. He would be swept up on the tide of black evolution. If Booker T. Washington could eat a sandwich in the president's house, he and Violet could make the city their own. The price of such ownership is high, however. In giving themselves over to their dream selves they become people neither recognizes: a childless couple, alienated from community in the big city.

Their problems could merely be the consequence of a weary familiarity which threatens any long marriage after years and years of sameness. But Morrison implicates the city in Joe and Violet's failings. Neither anticipated so much anguish in a city better than perfect. In essence, they are betrayed by the city's wonderful promise of perfection.

Morrison signals their recovery as a new affection for each other and for the city. Long hours of replenishing leisure replace obsessive work:

> They walk down 125th Street and across Seventh Avenue and if they get tired they sit down and rest on any stoop they want to and talk weather and youthful misbehavior to the woman leaning on the sill of the first-floor window. Or they saunter over to the Corner and join the crowd. . . . Once in a while they take the train all the way to 42nd Street to enjoy what Joe calls the stairway of the lions. Or they idle along 72nd Street to watch men dig holes in the ground for a new building. (223)

In the city they have found a sense of community and a way to be themselves. In Felice they have found a daughter. Older and saner, Joe and Violet are not what they imagined themselves, nor is the city what they imagined it to be. They can enjoy its excitement and opportunity without losing the best of their original selves. Perfection is not possible, but transcending imperfection is.

The New York that Morrison conceives is based upon the city's historical character as a final destination for southern blacks fleeing increasing discrimination and oppression, lynchings, and other violence against them during the early 1900s. They came in search of a refuge from want:

> Some were slow about it and traveled from Georgia to Illinois, to the City, back to Georgia, out to San Diego and finally, shaking their heads, surrendered themselves to the City. Others knew right away that it was for them, this City and no other. They came on a whim because there it was and why not? They came after much planning, many letters written to and from, to make sure and know how and how much and where. They came for a visit and forgot to go back to tall cotton or short. Discharged with or without honor, fired with or without notice, they hung around for a while and then could not imagine themselves anywhere else. Others came because a relative or hometown buddy said, "Man, you best see this place before you die"; or, "We got room now so pack your suitcase and don't bring no hightop shoes." (32)

Many who came did not find the mecca they sought. Work was not always available, and living conditions were sometimes miserable.

Morrison does not delineate these aspects of city life. They contribute to the novel's historical accuracy but not to its themes. Morrison is most concerned with developing the city's subjective, nonmaterial identity in the way that she develops identity of place throughout her work (the Bottom in *Sula*, a sultry Ohio community—on the periphery of a thriving segregated town—almost perversely surviving the effects of long-entrenched patterns of racism; Shalimar, Kentucky, in *Song of Solomon*, where women wear loose-fitting dresses and do not carry purses; they reflect a rural community and an inelegant, natural way of life; Isle des Chevalier with its primal forests and mythic undercurrents). In *Jazz* there is the seductive New York where "a colored man floats down out of the sky blowing a saxophone" (8) whose jazzy notes make one forget about "little pebbly creeks and apple trees . . ." (34). Children, men, and women like the Dumfrey sisters forget about southern origins. Graceful and "citified," the sisters have become "stuck up," having retreated from their beginnings in Cottown, Tennessee. In the city "they feel more like the people they always thought they were" (35); they feel "stronger," "riskier" (33).

One of Morrison's metaphors for the city's bewitching magnetism is its night sky—not the starry expanse that can be observed on a clear evening in the country, but a starless interior space "booming over a glittering city" (35). Sometimes it "can go purple and keep an orange heart . . ." imparting to everyone on the street below an enchanting glow. Most often, however, its oceanic depths are dark and mesmerizing. Contemplating this darkness is like penetrating to the city's soul, which is both unfathomable and revealing, both "welcoming and defensive at the same time" (9). Morrison does not say it, but perhaps it is these contradictory, competing messages that confuse people and make them "think they can do what they want and get away with it" (8) in the city. Perhaps it is the lack of certainty that gives them a sense of possibility and informs their stronger, riskier selves. Subliminally, the city sky infects the psyche in much the same way the phases of a moon are thought to affect personality and behavior. Throughout the novel Morrison back- and foregrounds her characters with images of city sky. During the late afternoons when Joe, for example, meets Dorcas, "the Iroquois sky . . . crayon-colors their love" (38). And by evening, at the end of their lovemaking, "the citysky is changing its orange heart to black" (38), becoming an accomplice to Joe's uncharacteristic daring.

The other metaphor for the city's mystique is music, which permeates the narrative in subtle but haunting ways. It is, to borrow a phrase, the music of the night, "the lowdown stuff" (56) played by "men in shirtsleeves [who] propped themselves in window frames, or clustered on rooftops, in alleyways, on stoops and in the apartments of relatives . . ." (58). It is the powerful blues of the 1920s, which insinuates itself into the brain until called into service to chronicle a transgression or to explain life itself. Everywhere the "belt-buckle tunes [were] vibrating from pianos and spinning on every Victrola. . . . There was no place to be where somewhere, close by, somebody was not . . . tickling the ivories, beating his skins, blowing off his horn while a knowing woman sang ain't nobody going to keep me down you got the right key but the wrong keyhole you got to get it bring it and put it right here, or else" (59–60) or where "a woman with a baby on her shoulder and a skillet in her hand" might sing "turn to my pillow where my sweet man used to be . . . how long, how long, how long" (56).

Like the city the music sends competing messages. It is simultaneously happy and hostile. While its "sooty" rhythms invite a correspondingly rhythmic response (headshake, footpat, dance step), its lyrics register complaint. Even the raunchy, edgy humor in lines like "hit me but don't quit me" (59) and "when I was young and in my prime I could get my barbecue any old time" (60) belies a subtext of lamentation. The music's excitement masks a "complicated anger" of wronged lovers, of betrayed veterans of World War I who returned from war in Europe to white violence, and of a generally disillusioned existence. But the music also registers audacious endurance. Under the influence of the music, people do "unwise disorderly things" (58): the music may have been responsible for the confusion in Joe's thoughts on the Saturday he tracked Dorcas to a room with someone else and shot her. The music also shaped Violet's attempt "to do something bluesy, something hep" like assaulting a dead girl. It was the "seeping music" of the city "that begged and challenged [Dorcas] each and every day. 'Come,' it said 'Come and do wrong'" (67).

All of the facets of New York—its excitement, its promise of a better life, its seduction, its repressed hostility and blue mood—coalesce in the personality of Morrison's unidentified narrator. She (slight textual clues and strong intuition points towards the narrator's identity as feminine) is the voice of the city: sassy, gossipy, prescient, and more. "I'm crazy about this City," she declares early in the novel (7). "A city like this one makes me dream tall and feel in on things. Hep" (7), she continues. From this point forward, she interprets the city with intimacy and understanding, describing the physical and nonphysical landscape, its past and present, advising of its dangers and attractions, commenting upon the lives of its inhabitants. She knows the city uptown where "wealthy whites, and plain ones too, pile into mansions" (8) as well as she knows it downtown on Lenox Avenue where "everything you want is right where you are; the church . . . the party . . . the bootleg houses . . . the beauty parlors, the barbershops, the juke joints . . . the number runner . . . brotherhood [and] sisterhood . . ." (10). The city, she admits, is not "pretty" (8), but it can be hospitable if one is "clever" (9) enough to figure it out. "Do what you please in the City, it is there to back and frame you no matter what you do. . . . All you have to do is heed the design—the way it's laid out for you, considerate, mindful of where you want to go and what you might need tomorrow" (9). She warns, however, that those who cannot decipher its design and avoid pitfalls lose their way and (literally and metaphorically) "end up out of control" (9) as Joe and Violet are for a time.

The narrator's observations are sometimes made as a disembodied consciousness whose perspective of city life is without borders: "When I look over strips of green grass lining the river, at church steeples and into the cream-and-copper halls of apartment buildings, I'm strong. Alone, yes, but top-notch and indestructible—like the City in 1926 when all the wars are over and there will never be another one. The people down there in the shadow are happy about that" (7), she confides. From somewhere above and beyond, the narrator's ubiquitous field of view distinguishes her from the people and things she observes "down there"; she knows more and sees more. Her view of the city is integrated, authoritative.

And yet, Morrison's narrator is not omniscient or infallible (all wars were not over in 1926). On the contrary, as a first person narrator, at times she seems to be a character participating in the sequence of events and interacting with other characters. In the opening lines of the novel she introduces Violet and Joe in a familiar, colloquial voice, admitting that "I know that woman. She used to live with a flock of birds on Lenox Avenue. Know her husband too" (3). Like a neighbor or acquaintance with recriminating secret details of a scandal, the narrator recounts a complete story of alienation, seduction, and violence, intermittently interjecting her uncharitable judgments: Violet is "skinny" and "mean"; Dorcas is "hardheaded as well as sly"; Joe is a "rat," or sometimes she takes a kinder view of him as a "nice, neighborly, everybody-knows-him man" (73); and Alice Manfred is repressed. Such conclusions are drawn from the narrator's apparent involvement in the day-to-day experience of these characters. She comments as if she is one of the crowd gathering to look on as Violet sits in the street or as one in the church as Violet crashes the funeral or as one of the flirting ladies attending lunch at Alice's house the day Joe comes to sell his beauty products and takes notice of Dorcas for the first time. "If I remember right," she says, "that October lunch in Alice Manfred's house, something was off" (71). She continues with a review of the eating, conversation, and personalities in a detailed but speculative way. She thinks Alice was "probably" distracted about Dorcas during lunch that day because, as she says, "I always believed that girl [Dorcas] was a pack of lies. . . . Maybe back in October Alice was beginning to think so too" (72). She wonders also if Alice "had a premonition of Joe Trace knocking on her door" (72) and desiring her niece. The narrator has many questions but few answers. As any other at that lunch might do, she theorizes about what happened. The narrator's point of view is often restricted to time and place. In such instances she is left to imagine, to doubt, to think about, to express an opinion, or even to admit that she does not know.

The dichotomy of her narrator's identity—as omnipresent on the one hand and as restricted to what she directly observes on the other—is new for Morrison, who in previous novels serves as storyteller relating events and point of view, free to move and to comment at will. The narrative perspective in *Jazz*, however, is more complex. Events are narrated in the first person even though the narrator is not a character. And although the narrator is free to move and comment at will, her comments are not always reliable. She compares her narrative force to the eye of a storm: as narrator she is at the center of storytelling; she gives it momentum—controls sequence, shapes perspective, manipulates meaning. Her characters are like "hens starving on rooftops," awaiting a rescue. "Figuring out what can be done to save them since they cannot save themselves" (219) is her responsibility. "It's my storm," she declares. "I break lives to prove I can mend them back again. And although the pain is theirs, I share it, don't I?" (219). The answer to that question is no, she does not. At the conclusion of her story the narrator confesses that she has little control over her characters' lives. At every turn "they contradicted" (280) her. She "invented stories about them—and doing it seemed . . . so fine" (220). She was certain, for example, that either Joe or Violet "would kill the other." She prepared herself and the reader for their violence. But they were too "busy being original, complicated, changeable—human" (220) to be so predictable, so easily manipulated. It never occurred to the narrator that her characters "were thinking other thoughts, feeling other feelings, putting their lives together in ways [she] never dreamed of" (221). The narrator's "know-it-all self" is really a fallacy. In the end she faces this deception; she is capable of psychological growth.

Clearly, Morrison's narrative voice in *Jazz* is a personification of the impersonal authorial voice. It is not the voice of the author occasionally stepping outside her role as omniscient observer to contribute an opinion—an awkward intrusion at best. It is the author incarnating—as a God might take on human form—as fictional muscle and bone, giving herself a consciousness and presence in the text. She does not interact, but she exists in a parallel space, chronicling Joe and Violet's story, and to some extent telling her own. She characterizes herself as introverted, living "a long time in . . . [her] own mind . . . close[ing] [herself] off in places . . ." (9), but longing for the kind of public affection Joe and Violet have found in the calm after their storm. When she gives up authorial powers for personal identity in the text, the narrator, like other characters, is subject to the aspirations and urges of humankind.

Morrison's personification of the impersonal authorial voice dramatizes the undivined aspect of the creative-writing process. During the course of composing, minor plots and characters may take on an unexpected primary focus as planned themes recede and vice versa. Mark Twain's familiar account of what happened to the musical twins who started out headlining his novel *Pudd'nhead Wilson* facetiously illustrates the point. The novel's original title was *Those Extraordinary Twins,* but somewhere in the composition process their story was subsumed by another. Twain explains:

> I meant to make it very short. . . . But the tale kept spreading along, and spreading along, and other people got to intruding themselves and taking up more and more room with their talk and their affairs. . . .
> When the book was finished and I came to look around to see what had become of the team I had originally started out with . . . they had disappeared from the story some time or other. I hunted about and found them . . . stranded, idle, forgotten, and permanently useless.[4]

Kate Chopin's tongue-in-cheek response to criticism of *The Awakening* is similar. Censored for Edna Pontellier's decision to leave her husband and children to seek fulfillment as a woman and artist, Chopin says, "I thought it might be entertaining (to myself) to throw them together and see what would happen. I never dreamed of Mrs. Pontellier making such a mess of things and working out her own damnation as she did. If I had had the slightest intimation of such a thing I would have excluded her from the company. But when I found out what she was up to, the play was half over and it was then too late."[5] Morrison's view of a writer's relationship to her characters is expressed in less cavalier terms than Twain's and Chopin's views. Her characters are "very carefully imagined." She knows "all there is to know about them." She knows that they "have nothing on their minds but themselves" and are capable of getting out of a writer's hands. But Morrison feels that "you can't let them write your book for you."[6] She does not give up authorial control because that would mean a sacrifice of her art. And yet, she does have a regard for the unanticipated quality of writing. Without losing sight of her controlling image,[7] Morrison does not fear the tough choices that her characters sometimes compel her to make for them if she is to write truthfully about them. To some spiritual extent it is her characters and not she who write books, and she must follow the story path where they lead. She has been chosen by them to represent them, to tell their stories, exhibit their experience.

This relationship between author and subject[s] shapes Morrison's conception of narrator in *Jazz*. Like Morrison the narrator is charged with interpreting and presenting the truth of her character's lives, and like Morrison she must be intuitive enough to receive these truths (the narrator as storyteller mirrors Morrison as storyteller). If she is not, the characters create their own reality in spite of her, and the narrative is false. (Of course, as author Morrison has more leeway here. Without her, her characters have no recourse. They must live with her failure.) "What was I thinking of?" (160), the narrator asks after failing to perceive a character's true motivation. "How could I have imagined him so poorly? . . . I have been careless and stupid and it infuriates me to discover (again) how unreliable I am" (160). She resolves to be more attentive in the future: "Now I have to think this through, carefully, even though I may be doomed to another misunderstanding. I have to do it and not break down" (161). She "want[s] to be the language that wishes him well, speaks his name, wakes him when his eyes need to be open" (161). Her language will construct his experience. Unfortunately, the narrator repeats her failures—with other characters. Hers is a process of trial and error, like an artful jazz improvisation inventing itself from a stated music theme which, indeed, was Morrison's controlling image of *Jazz* as she composed it: a book "writing itself. Imagining itself. Talking. Aware of what it is doing," willing "to fail, to be wrong" like a jazz performance.[8] *Jazz*, Morrison says, "predicts its own story. Sometimes it is wrong because of faulty vision. It simply did not imagine those characters well enough, admits it was wrong, and the characters talk back the way jazz musicians do. It has to listen to the characters it has invented, and then learn something from them."[9]

It also listens to, or is certainly aware of, its audience. In that sense *Jazz* advances Morrison's ideas about the reader's participation in making meaning in her novels. The text should promote complicity, Morrison believes, between author and reader. It should elicit the reader's interpretation and activate her imagination. That is the narrator's missive to readers in the final lines of the novel. Having provided a parting view of Joe and Violet in denouement—a calm loving after their storm—the narrator turns to the reader with a declaration of intimate vulnerability: I have . . . surrendered my whole self reckless to you . . . . I love the way you hold me, how close you let me be to you. I like your fingers on and on, lifting, turning. I have watched your face for a long time now, and missed your eyes when you went away from me. Talking to you and hearing you answer—that's the kick (229). An act of reading rendered as a act of lovemaking becomes a moment of mutual creation. You may chose to "make me, remake me," the narrator concludes, and "I am free to let you" (229). That is the reader's privilege and the author's promise.

Notes

1. Morrison has written that she is committed to *in medias res* openings in her novels because she is interested in how things happen, who did what, and why. She therefore puts the significant details up front to entice the reader into wanting to know the rest of the story. See Morrison, "Unspeakable Things Unspoken: The Afro-American Presence in American Literature," *Michigan Quarterly Review* 28 (Winter 1989): 1–34; and Elissa Schappell and Claudia Brodsky Lacour, "Toni Morrison: The Art of Fiction," *Paris Review* 128 (Fall 1993) 85–125.

2. Nellie Y. McKay, "Interview with Toni Morrison," *Contemporary Literature* 24 (Winter 1983): 413–29. Rpt. in *Toni Morrison: Critical Perspectives Past and Present*, ed. Henry Louis Gates, Jr., and K. A. Appiah (New York: Amistad, 1993) 405.

3. Toni Morrison, *Jazz* (New York: Alfred A. Knopf, 1992) 73. Subsequent references will appear in parentheses in the text.

4. Mark Twain, *Pudd'nhead Wilson*, ed. with an introduction by Malcolm Bradbury (New York: Penguin, 1969) 230–31.

5. Per Seyersted, *Kate Chopin: A Critical Biography* (Baton Rouge: Louisiana State University Press) 176.

6. Schappell and Lacour 106.

7. In her interview with Schappell and Lacour, Morrison talks about the visual images that control the structure of each novel's focus as she writes.

8. Schappell and Lacour 116.

9. Schappell and Lacour 117.

7

LITERARY AND SOCIAL CRITICISM
PLAYING IN THE DARK

Since 1974 Morrison's essays and interviews have comprised a reservoir of ideas about American culture. Over the years she has spoken and written about issues of race, class, and gender and how they shape perception and identity in American society. Of course, in the broadest sense these are also the subjects of her novels. And because this connection exists between her fiction and nonfiction, it is possible, even desirable, to read one as a clarifying vision of the other. Indeed, in some cases Morrison's comments are extensive tutorials on meaning in her novels. But even when the relationship between her fiction and nonfiction is not absolute, a consistent thread of philosophical, literary, political, and cultural thought connects her writing.

Playing in the Dark, a recent work of nonfiction concerned with the way race and gender have defined American literature and life, illustrates this consistency. It is Morrison's most thorough treatment of these matters. It is a culmination of academic inquiry and scholarship that grew out of a course that Morrison teaches in American literature at Princeton, and it explores ideas discussed in three William E. Massey, Sr., lectures given at Harvard. The result of her endeavors has been, according to Morrison, the emergence of a keen interest "in the way black people ignite critical moments of discovery or change or emphasis in literature not written by them."[1] Morrison has kept a file on such moments, which have largely been underremarked by critics but which she believes deserve examination. In the preface to *Playing in the Dark,* Morrison recalls making an addition to her file of critical moments after reading Marie Cardinal's account of her descent into insanity in *The Words To Say It*. Morrison is intrigued by Cardinal's description of her anxiety attack at age nineteen or twenty during a Louis Armstrong concert. Cardinal recalls that "my heart began to accelerate, becoming more important than the music, shaking the bars of my rib cage, compressing my lungs so the air could no longer enter them. Gripped by panic at the idea of dying there in the middle of spasms, stomping feet, and the crowd howling, I ran into the street like someone possessed" (vii). Morrison finds the "clarity" of Cardinal's recollection noteworthy. But she also asks, with eyebrows raised, "What on earth was Louie playing that night?" (vii). And then, more to her point, she wonders whether some other music—an Edith Piaf concert or an Antonín Dvorak composition—would have affected Cardinal with such force or whether the "cultural associations of Jazz" with blackness were the active ingredients responsible for precipitating Cardinal's anxiety. Morrison speculates that although "either [Piaf's or Dvorak's music] *could* have" (viii; emphasis added), it is significant that Armstrong's did. For a Frenchwoman born in Algeria, not surprisingly simultaneously repulsed and attracted by Arab (nonwhite) images, the exotic figurations of jazz perhaps possessed the power to unlock her subconscious and unleash its force.

Morrison believes that a writer's cultural and personal history undoubtedly shapes her work. This process is obvious in Cardinal's case: her narrative is an imaginative rendering of her life, her history. Fiction writers too are subject to historical influence, and according to Morrison, in no context is that influence more demonstrable than in nineteenth- and twentieth-century American literature where literary character and themes mirror life in America. Morrison is particularly concerned with the way literature reflects a racialized society—not in the recognizable way blacks are marginalized in texts (as they are in society) to provide local color or "a needed moral gesture, humor, or bit of pathos" (15), but in a more systemic, pathological way. "The major and championed characteristics of our national literature—individualism, masculinity, social engagement versus historical isolation; acute and ambiguous moral problematics; the thematics of innocence coupled with an obsession with figurations of death and hell," are, Morrison suggests, responses to a black presence (5). Over four hundred years of black suffusion (first African and later African-American) in all aspects of life in the United States has a corresponding infusion of black images in literature. Morrison calls the presence of these images "American Africanism." It is the white writer's self-conscious and unconscious use of blackness that results from life in a society where racial identity dominates thinking and pervades the literary imagination as well. Any nonblack writer who perpetuates the ideology of "racial hierarchy, racial exclusion, and racial vulnerability and availability" (11) most likely makes use of Africanism.

Morrison traces Africanism from its early appearance in eighteenth-century personal narrative to its use in contemporary fictional narrative—from William Dunbar, an educated Scottish émigré to the American colonies, to Poe, Twain, and Cather, and finally to Hemingway. Dunbar's letters and diary, sketching in his life as a Mississippi planter and slaveholder, reveal much about the psychological use white European settlers made of black slaves in their sojourn toward power, authority, and authenticity. Absolute control over others' lives was exalting and empowering, and the result was the emergence of Dunbar (and slaveholders like him) as a "distinctive new man, a borderland gentleman, a man of property in a raw, half-savage world."[2] Blacks provided the contrast that made this identity of a new American possible, Morrison thinks. Their abjectness heightened the ful-fillment derived from dominating them in the way that any desirable con-dition is made more so by fear of its opposite. Morrison proposes that the white population convinced itself that the slave population had offered itself up as surrogate selves for meditation on problems of freedom, failure, aggression, evil, sin, and greed. Americans did not have a "predatory" (47) noble class to struggle against and to counter its view of itself as morally good. (Only such a counterpoint could unify national character, by giving Americans a point of resistance.) Without a corrupt nobility they turned for a counterpoint to the black population, which offered an ideological and visible basis for contrast. "For in that construction of blackness *and* enslavement," says Morrison, "could be found not only the not-free but also, with the dramatic polarity created by skin color, the projection of the not-me. The result was a playground for the imagination" (38). (Presum-ably, Morrison views the American fight with Britain as having no signifi-cant bearing on this argument. That war may be seen as a generic struggle for the rights of white men that informs the national spirit of indepen-dence, but it does not inform the aspect of national character—aristocratic privilege and license—that emanates from a sense of moral goodness; a black presence provided that identity.)

In consequence, a black presence is inextricably and uncomfortably bound to the American character, and Morrison sees this amalgam sharply reflected in the literature from its origins to its present. As it has been in society historically, in literature, blacks are not accorded full stature as agents of their own fictional destinies. Instead, the black character is reliably one dimensional, and the black experience created by the white imagination is reduced to Africanism: stereotypical personae; symbols of otherness (immorality, ignorance, cowardice, enslavement, servility, savagery); objects of humor; or in the absence of black character and experience, a "deep abiding" darkness that pervades the narrative.

Morrison illustrates her meaning in abbreviated analyses of Twain's *Huckleberry Finn*, Cather's *Sapphira and the Slave Girl*, Poe's *Narrative of Arthur Gordon Pym*, and Hemingway's *To Have and Have Not*. In reviewing the much-discussed final chapters of *Huckleberry Finn*, Morrison declares Jim's failed bid for freedom, his (re)enslavement, to be a perfect complement to Huck's liberty. The latter cannot be comprehended without the former. She supplements the prevailing and opposing views which explain the novel's ending (when Tom's romantic machinations reemerge to overshadow Huck's moral growth and Jim's integrity) as either evidence of Twain's deterioration as an artist or as a lesson in real life. In addition to these interpretations, Morrison proposes that the ending be seen as Twain's unconscious adaptation of the meaning of a black presence. The ending is "the elaborate deferment of a necessary and necessarily unfree Africanist character's escape because freedom has no meaning to Huck or to the text without the specter of enslavement, the anodyne to individualism; the yardstick of absolute power over the life of another; the signed, marked, informing, and mutating presence of a black slave" (56). Morrison makes in essence the same point about each writer whose work she discusses. Each is subject to, for the most part, unexamined ideas about race that taint the imagination and sabotage the writer's text.

Morrison approaches this study of America's literary imagination from a writer's perspective and not from an academic critic's. She is, not unfairly, accused of handling the language and work of criticism clumsily here,[3] but she says early in *Playing in the Dark* that she does "not bring to these matters solely or even principally the tools of a literary critic" (3). Rather, as a writer, she is interested in the way writers develop their subjects and the conscious, but especially the unconscious literary strategies they employ. Experience determines these strategies, and in a racialized society racial symbols are a convenient literary shorthand. "The presence of black people is inherent . . . in the earliest lesson every child is taught regarding his or her distinctiveness," Morrison asserts. "Africanism is inextricable from the definition of Americanness" (65), she continues, and from the metaphorical (re)presentation of national character.

Morrison has never been tempted to the metaphorical and metaphysi-
cal use of race in her fiction. Obviously, she is not inclined to embrace a
literary tradition that may promote "racial superiority, cultural hegemony,
and dismissive 'othering' of people . . ." (x). Resisting temptation, Morrison
wishes to "free up the language from its sometimes sinister, frequently lazy,
almost always predictable employment of racially informed and determined
chains" (xv).

"Recitatif," the only short story Morrison has written, is an experi-
ment in communicating without using racial codes as a shortcut. The narrative, which Morrison describes (in the preface to *Playing in the Dark*) as
a story "about two characters of different races for whom racial identity is
crucial" (xi), deftly avoids racial stereotyping. In the story eight-year-old
girls develop bonds of friendship and trust during four months that both
are placed temporarily at St. Bonaventure, an orphanage. Initially, divided
by their differences—Twyla, the first-person speaker, protests being "stuck
in a strange place with a girl from a whole other race"[4]—the girls quickly
find an ally in each other. Mutual need neutralizes race hatred and makes
their similarities much more important than their differences. Unlike the
other children at St. Bonaventure, the girls are not "real orphans with beautiful dead parents in the sky"(244). In place of these, Twyla and Roberta
have dysfunctional living mothers: one is neglectful, and the other suffers
from mental illness. For this and for being poor students, they are ostracized and so have only each other as companions. Together they endure
intimidation from older girls on the second floor and by other girls at the
orphanage who taunt them with the names salt and pepper. Together they
spy on the big girls and occasionally watch helplessly when they harass
Maggie, a mute woman who works in the kitchen at the orphanage.

Morrison does not reveal which of the girls is black and which is white,
and yet, as she says, racial identity is crucial. It not only defines her characters' relationship to each other, but it locates that relationship within
America's successive and changing epochs of racial disharmony from the
late 1950s through the early 1980s. In the 1950s the petty prejudices at
the orphanage prove to be innocuous, and the girls easily transcend these
in their girlhood need for companionship. Even when Roberta's mother
insults Twyla's by refusing to greet her on visitor's day (and Twyla's mother
responds with name-calling), the girls are able to dissociate the women's
behavior from the affection of their own relationship. When Roberta leaves
the orphanage to go back to her mother, the girls promise to keep in touch,

but time fades memories. Many years later, during a chance meeting at Howard Johnson's, where Twyla waits tables and Roberta is passing through, the girls, now women, are essentially strangers swept up in the strife of the 1960s. This time it is Twyla who is naive and Roberta who is wise to the ways of the world. With her "big and wild hair," "earrings the size of bracelets" (253), and heavy makeup, Roberta has traveled too far from the orphanage to acknowledge a past that included an unhip uniformed waitress who does not know who Jimi Hendrix is. In the present they are just "a black girl and a white girl meeting in a Howard Johnson's on the road and nothing to say" (253).

Twelve years later the women, since married, meet again at a supermarket in an affluent suburb where Roberta lives with her wealthy husband and where Twyla occasionally shops even though on the salary of her husband, a fireman, she cannot afford the fancy groceries marketed there. Over coffee they are reconciled, "behaving like sisters separated for much too long" (253). Time has no rational meaning for them. Just as a few moments had veiled them from each other in the Howard Johnson's years earlier, now "in just a pulse beat, twenty years disappeared and all of it came rushing back" (253)—until in the act of recall, Roberta encourages Twyla to remember the day the big girls at the orphanage pushed Maggie, the woman from the kitchen, and tore her clothes as the two younger girls watched. Twyla is disturbed because her memory's version of the event is less malevolent: Maggie fell and the other girls laughed. The conflicting narratives produce a rupture that each feels but that neither acknowledges. The rupture deepens into an impassable divide a few years later when the two face each other from opposite sides of a school busing issue. Twyla accuses Roberta of bigotry for opposing busing, and Roberta hurls a more astonishing accusation: Maggie was black, and Twyla, Roberta asserts, had kicked her when the other girls pushed her to the ground. In a confrontation at the picket line, Roberta charges Twyla with being "the same little state kid who kicked a poor old black lady when she was down on the ground. You kicked a black lady," Roberta continues, "and you have the nerve to call me a bigot" (257). Twyla rejects both counts: that Maggie was black and that she assaulted her.

This exchange is typical of the racial dystopia Morrison devises for her characters and for her readers. The orphanage was an unlikely cover of protection for the unfettered intimacy each girl felt with the other. Later, in adulthood, where new alliances are possible—husband, friends, children—

the hothouse intimacy of the orphanage is impossible between a black woman and a white woman. The utopian past becomes the dystopic present of shattered memories.

Morrison's readers experience a kind of dystopia as well, if one may view Morrison's deliberate and clever misappropriation of racial stereotype as a dystopic condition for readers accustomed to stereotypes. In "Recitatif" racial identities are shifting and elusive. The reader cannot draw easy conclusions. Some readers may be tempted, for example, to deduce that Twyla is echoing white stereotypes of blacks when she says that they (and Roberta) never wash their hair and they smell funny and to deduce that Roberta's big hair style at the Howard Johnson's is an Afro and Roberta must therefore be black. Other readers, however, may believe that only as a white woman could Roberta outpace Twyla socially and financially. Only a white woman could plausibly live so well, with an affluent husband who affords a driver and servants. Only a white woman could demonstrate on the street against school busing since most blacks saw it as Twyla does—an opportunity for children of both races to be better educated. And yet, why would Twyla, if she is black, kick Maggie, who is one of her own? Questions beget questions in Morrison's text, and all require strenuous consideration. Despite most reader's wishes to assess, settle, draw conclusions, Morrison is resolute in requiring readers to participate in creating meaning. She will offer no convenient stereotypes as shortcuts.

Morrison does not resolve the dilemma of Maggie's racial identity, but in the final exchange between her characters—another chance meeting in a coffee shop on Christmas Eve many years after the busing conflict—whether Maggie is black or white is irrelevant. For Twyla and Roberta, Maggie was a symbol of defeat, a reminder of their own helplessness. Being deaf, mute, and a victim is what they both remember about Maggie and what they both hated about her. Neither had kicked the old woman, but both had wanted to. The burden of their young lives was bearable when pain, transformed to anger, was shifted to Maggie. Without realizing it, however, in hating Maggie, they hated themselves and each other. Now, after many years, they face the guilt over that anger and having done so can forgive each other and review the past truthfully, remembering Maggie not defensively, but empathetically, as Roberta urgently wonders "What the hell happened to Maggie?" (261).

By the time this question is asked, the storm over race has passed. Morrison had momentarily raised the familiar specter of race prejudice, and just as the reader took a relaxing breath, grateful finally for the sure footing of predictable stereotype, Morrison changed direction. She is not interested in bigotry, but in humanity, lost and found. Maggie is not the Africanist set piece that Morrison decries.

Morrison shuns Africanism, but too many authors have not. *Playing in the Dark* puts the spotlight on some of those who have not and delineates what Morrison believes is the underexamined and overlooked subtext of race that imprints the literary canon of America.[5] Despite gaps in her discourse (she does not account for Indians as a dark presence in the literature of early America, and her examination of text is too brief and too arbitrary to allow her to make anything but speculative conclusions), Morrison's review is preliminary to the kind of penetrating exploration of the canon that she invites.

Notes

1. Toni Morrison, *Playing in the Dark: Whiteness and the Literary Imagination* (Cambridge: Harvard University Press, 1992) viii. Subsequent references will appear in parentheses in the text.

2. Morrison is quoting Bernard Bailyn, *Voyagers to the West: A Passage in the Peopling of America on the Eve of the Revolution* (New York: Alfred A. Knopf, 1986) 488–92.

3. See Mark Edmundson, "Literature in Living Color," *Book World* (7 June 1992).

4. Toni Morrison, "Recitatif," *Confirmation: An Anthology of African American Woman*, ed. Amiri Baraka and Amina Baraka (New York: William Morrow, 1983) xi.

5. Morrison is also interested in the way race perverts the American character and the American mind. In her introduction to *Race[ing] Justice, [En]gender[ing] Power: Essays on Anita Hill, Clarence Thomas, and the Construction of Social Reality* (New York: Pantheon, 1992), she gives an unflinching analysis of the consequences of cultural hegemony on the body politic. In discussing the Clarence Thomas confirmation hearings, Morrison discerns in the entire episode—from nomination to confirmation—patterns of dysfunction related to race, gender, and class. The spectacle of the hearings was tolerated only because the agents were black, says Morrison, and because the charges by Hill and countercharges by Thomas evoked two black stereotypes with which the country is familiar, even comfortable: the sexually aggressive black male and sexually easy black female. These and other stereotypes, Morrison believes, provided an unofficial narrative, a subtext, to the official narrative of the proceedings and for the observant, this subtext of racial stereotype effectively undermined and wholly invalidated the official narrative.

CONCLUSION

Language as a symbol of culture is especially Morrison's concern. She is keenly interested in the authentic and authenticating language of public narrative (in literature, politics, society), a point which she makes eloquently in her Nobel Prize lecture to the Swedish Academy. The lecture is an ode to language, the essential conduit of knowledge between individuals and generations. Language is the building block of narrative with which the artist inexplicably, illuminatingly weaves together the past, present, and future experiences of life. Narrative bequeaths continuity. Narrative language is continually threatened, however, by narrow thinking which reduces rather than creates, which excludes rather than includes, which shrouds rather that illuminates. Morrison's work opposes these threats as it elevates narrative language to heights of truth and understanding. To use Morrison's own words spoken in praise of another, her "word-work is sublime . . . because it is generative"[1] and not reductive.

In the narrative of her Nobel Prize lecture, Morrison chronicles the dangers of language abuse and misuse and celebrates the language of hope and possibility. Beginning with the standard narrative opening "once upon a time," which may be, according to Morrison, "the oldest sentence in the world and the earliest one we remember from childhood" (7), she recalls a fable familiar to her in many cultural variations. Choosing a version that reflects her cultural background, Morrison relates that a wise old woman, the daughter of African slaves, is asked by a gathering of young people to demonstrate her wisdom by saying whether the bird they hold is alive or dead. After considerable reflection the woman answers "I don't know whether the bird you are holding is dead or alive, but what I do know is that it is in your hands" (11). Fascinated by the significance of the children's question and the woman's response, Morrison (again reflecting her own interests and work) "choose[s] to read the bird as language and the woman as a practiced writer" (12). In that context the old woman's response acknowledges the responsibility that all users of language have for its death and for its survival. Language that does not ask questions "cannot form or tolerate new ideas . . . [cannot] tell another story" (14) and is dead. Language that "reach[es] toward the ineffable . . . [and that] surges toward knowledge, lives" (21). The children hear the old woman and ask more questions, but this second time their questions are less arrogant than pleading. This time they do not brandish their own limited knowledge as a weapon to defeat her wisdom. Understanding more about the transforming force of narrative, they say

> Tell us what it is to be a woman so that we may know what it is to be a man. What moves at the margin. What it is to have no home in this place. To be set adrift from the one you knew. What it is to live at the edge of towns that cannot bear your company. Tell us about ships turned away from shorelines at Easter, placenta in a field. Tell us about a wagonload of slaves, how they sang so softly their breath was indistinguishable from the falling snow. How they knew from the hunch of the nearest shoulder that the next stop would be their last. How, with hands prayered in their sex, they thought of heat, then sun. Lifting their faces as though it was there for the taking. They stop at an inn. The driver and his mate go in with the lamp, leaving them humming in the dark. The horse's void stems into the snow beneath its hooves and the hiss and melt are the envy of the freezing slaves.
>
> The inn door opens: a girl and a boy step away from its light. They climb into the wagon bed. The boy will have a gun in three years, but now he carries a lamp and a jug of warm cider. They pass it from mouth to mouth. The girl offers bread, pieces of meat and something more: a glance into the eyes of the one she serves. One helping for each man, two for each woman. And a look. They look back. The next stop will be their last. But not this one. This one is warmed. (28–30)

Narrative, stories, links the past with the present and with a future. In weaving a narrative of cultural history, the old woman, whom Morrison envisions as a practiced writer, gives the young people in her audience a knowledge of the past on which to construct their future experiences. Like the old woman Morrison, herself a practiced writer, also weaves stories which bridge eras and generations. In her hands the language lives as extraordinary narratives of the humanity of her people.

Note

1. Toni Morrison, "Lecture and Speech of Acceptance, Upon the Award of the Nobel Prize for Literature, *The Nobel Lecture in Literature* (New York: Alfred A. Knopf, 1993) 22. Subsequent references appear in parenthesis.

Selected Bibliography

Novels

The Bluest Eye. New York: Holt, Rinehart and Winston, 1970. London: Chatto & Windus, 1979.

Sula. New York: Alfred A. Knopf, 1973. London: Allen Lane, 1974.

Song of Solomon. New York: Alfred A. Knopf, 1977. London: Chatto & Windus, 1978.

Tar Baby. New York: Alfred A. Knopf, 1981. London: Chatto & Windus, 1981.

Beloved. New York: Alfred A. Knopf, 1987. London: Chatto & Windus, 1987.

Jazz. New York: Alfred A. Knopf, 1992. London: Chatto & Windus, 1992.

Literary Criticism

Playing in the Dark: Whiteness and the Literary Imagination. Cambridge: Harvard University Press, 1992.

Edited Volume

Race[ing] Justice, [En]gender[ing] Power: Essays on Anita Hill, Clarence Thomas, and the Construction of Social Reality. New York: Pantheon, 1992.

Selected Uncollected Essays

"What the Black Woman Thinks About Women's Lib." *New York Times Magazine* 22 August 1971: 14ff.

"Behind the Making of the Black Book." *Black World* 23 (February 1974): 86–90.

"Rediscovering Black History." *New York Times Magazine* 11 August 1974: 14ff.

"A Slow Walk of Trees." *New York Times Magazine* 4 July 1976: 104ff

"Memory, Creation, and Writing." *Thought* 59 (December 1984): 385–90.

"Rootedness: The Ancestor as Foundation." *Black Women Writers (1950–1980).* Ed. Marie Evans. New York: Doubleday, 1984. 339–45.

"The Site of Memory." *Inventing the Truth: The Art and Craft of Memoir.* Ed. William Zinsser. Boston: Houghton Mifflin, 1987. 101–24.

"Unspeakable Things Unspoken: The Afro-American Presence in American Literature." *Michigan Quarterly Review* 28 (Winter 1989): 1–34.

"Lecture and Speech of Acceptance, Upon the Award of the Nobel Prize for Literature. *The Nobel Lecture in Literature.* New York: Alfred A. Knopf, 1994.

Selected Interviews

Carabi, Angels. "Toni Morrison." *Belle Lettres* (Winter 1994): 38–39; 86–90.

Davis, Christina. "Interview with Toni Morrison." *Presence Africaine* (First Quarterly, 1988). Rpt. in *Toni Morrison: Critical Perspectives Past and Present.* Ed. Henry Louis Gates, Jr., and K. A. Appiah. New York: Amistad, 1993.

Jones, Bessie W. "An Interview with Toni Morrison." *The World of Toni Morrison.* Ed. Bessie W. Jones and Audrey L. Vinson. Dubuque, Iowa: Kendall/Hunt, 1985.

LeClair, Thomas. "'The Language Must Not Sweat': A Conversation with Toni Morrison." *New Republic* 184 (21 March 1981): 25–30.

Lester, Rosemarie K. "An Interview with Toni Morrison, Hessian Radio Network, Frankfurt, West Germany." *Critical Essays on Toni Morrison.* Ed. Nellie Y. McKay. Boston: G. K. Hall & Co., 1988. 47–54.

McKay, Nellie Y. "An Interview with Toni Morrison." *Contemporary Literature* 24 (Winter 1983): 413–29. Rpt. in *Toni Morrison: Critical Perspectives Past and Present.* Ed. Henry Louis Gates, Jr., and K. A. Appiah. New York: Amistad, 1993.

Naylor, Gloria, and Toni Morrison. "A Conversation." *Southern Review* 21 (1985): 567–93.

Schappell, Elissa, and Claudia Brodsky Lacour. "Toni Morrison: The Art of Fiction." *Paris Review* 128 (Fall 1993): 83–125.

Stepto, Robert B. "Intimate Things in Place: A Conversation with Toni Morrison." *Massachusetts Review* 18 (Autumn 1977): 473–89. Rpt. in *Toni Morrison: Critical Perspectives Past and Present.* Ed. Henry Louis Gates, Jr., and K. A. Appiah. New York: Amistad, 1993.

Tate, Claudia. "Conversation with Toni Morrison." *Black Women Writers at Work.* Ed. Claudia Tate. New York: Continuum Publishing Co., 1983. 117–31.

Selected Critical Books, Collected Articles, and Special Journal Editions

Bjork, Patrick. *The Novels of Toni Morrison: The Search for Self and Place Within the Community.* New York: Lang, 1992. Discusses five novels and examines how cultural and communal values, beliefs, and customs contribute to the protagonists' search for identity and place.

Gates, Henry Louis, Jr., and K. A. Appiah, eds. *Toni Morrison: Critical Perspectives Past and Present.* Volume of reviews, interviews, previously published and new critical essays on Morrison's work. Extensive bibliography of critical books and essays.

Harris, Trudier. *Fiction and Folklore: The Novels of Toni Morrison.* Knoxville: University of Tennessee Press, 1991. Examines the folk traditions in Morrison's novels and proposes that Morrison goes beyond the casual use of folklore to a replication of the culture that gives rise to folk traditions. Devotes a chapter to each of Morrison's first five novels.

Heinz, Denise. *The Dilemma of "Double-Consciousness": Toni Morrison's Novels.* Athens: University of Georgia Press, 1993. Describes an ever-enlarging artistic perspective in Morrison's work which expands from the individual, to the family, community, and then to society.

Holloway, Karla F. C. and Stephanie A. Demetrakopoulous. *New Dimensions of Spirituality: A Biracial and Bicultural Reading of the Novels of Toni Morrison.* Westport, Connecticut: Greenwood Press, 1987. A subjective approach to a scholarly reading of Morrison's texts. Each author takes a turn interpreting novels in terms of her academic and cultural background.

Mbalia, Doreatha Drummond. *Toni Morrison's Developing Class Consciousness.* Selinsgrove, Pa.: Susquehanna University Press, 1991. Devotes a chapter to each of Morrison's novels, except *Jazz.* Treats each novel as a solution to some aspect of "oppression afflicting African people" and defines each novel as a reflection of Morrison's growing social consciousness.

McKay, Nellie, ed. *Critical Essays on Toni Morrison.* Boston: G. K. Hall, 1988. Interviews with Morrison, essays on her fiction, and selected reviews of her first four novels.

Otten, Terry. *The Crime of Innocence in the Fiction of Toni Morrison.* Columbia: University of Missouri Press, 1989. Compact and thoughtful examination of Morrison's evolving moral vision.

Samuels, Wilfred D., and Clenora Hudson-Weems. *Toni Morrison.* Boston: Twayne Publishers, 1990. Examines Morrison's narrative style and her theme of self-discovery.

Selected Critical Articles

Awkward, Michael. "'Unruly and Let Loose': Myth, Ideaology, and Gender in *Song of Solomon*." *Callaloo* 13 (Summer 1990): 482–98. Discusses Morrison's revision of African and Western myths in *Song of Solomon* which is seen to reflect, to an extent, feminist ideology.

———. "'The Evil of Fulfillment': Scapegoating and Narration in *The Bluest Eye*." *Inspiriting Influences, Tradition, Revision, and Afro-American Women's Novels*. New York: Columbia University Press, 1989. 57–95. Thoughtful discussion of Morrison's placement within the African American literary tradition.

Bakerman, Jane S. "Failures of Love: Female Initiation in the Novels of Toni Morrison." *American Literature* 52 (January 1981): 543–63. A problematic reading of female failure in *The Bluest Eye, Sula,* and *Song of Solomon.*

Blake, Susan L. "Folklore and Community in *Song of Solomon*." *Melus* 7 (1980): 77–82. Sees Milkman's journey in *Song of Solomon* as not only a discovery of individual and family identity but as an essential discovery of community.

Bryant, Cedric Gael. "The Orderliness of Disorder: Madness and Evil in Toni Morrison's *Sula*." *Black American Literature Forum* 24 (Winter 1990): 731–45. Discussion of the balanced tension between unsocialized individuals—those who are crazy, mentally deficient, evil—and the communities that keep them.

Christian, Barbara. "Community and Nature: The Novels of Toni Morrison." *Journal of Ethnic Studies* 7 (February 1980): 65–78. Examines Morrison's use of Nature (the land) to define community (place, setting) and character in *Sula, The Bluest Eye,* and *Song of Solomon.*

Coleman, Alisha R. "One and One Make One: A Metacritical and Psychoanalytic Reading of Friendship in Toni Morrison's *Sula*." *CLA Journal* 37 (December 1993): 145–55.

Coleman, James W. "The Quest for Wholeness in Toni Morrison's *Tar Baby*." *Black American Literature Forum* 20 (Spring/Summer 1986): 63–73. General discussion of the quest for identity in *Sula, The Bluest Eye, Song of Solomon* and *Tar Baby.*

Cowart, David. "Faulkner and Joyce in Morrison's *Song of Solomon*." *American Literature* 62 (March 1990): 87–100. Locates Morrison's accomplishment within a larger literary tradition.

Guerrero, Edward. "Tracking 'The Look' in the Novels of Toni Morrison." *Black American Literature Forum* 24 (Winter 1990): 761–73. Explores Morrison's delineation of white male standards of beauty in her first five novels.

Halloway, Karla F. C. "*Beloved*: A Spiritual." *Callaloo* 13 (1990): 516–25. Sees *Beloved* as a revision of the historical record of black women's experiences.

Examines the literary devices Morrison uses to transform one woman's history into cultural myth.

Harris, A. Leslie. "Myth and Structure in Toni Morrison's *Song of Solomon*." *Melus* 7 (Fall 1980): 69–76. Finds myth in *Song of Solomon* to be a universalizing force which broadens the novel's appeal.

Lee, Dorothy H. "The Quest for Self: Triumph and Failure in the Works of Toni Morrison." In *Black Women Writers (1950–1980): A Critical Evaluation*. Ed. Marie Evans; Intro. Stephen E. Henderson. (Garden City, N. Y.: Anchor-Doubleday, 1984): 346–60. Approaches each of Morrison's first four novels as a variation on Morrison's singular concern with the relationship between community and the individual quest for identity; sees the quest as an organizing principle in Morrison's work.

Montgomery, Maxin Lavon. "A Pilgrimage to the Origins: The Apocalypse as Structure and Theme in Toni Morrison's *Sula*." *Black American Literature Forum* 23 (Spring 1989): 127–37. Proposes that although catastrophe abounds in *Sula*, it is not a signal of defeat as it is in the Western apocalyptic vision, but is an opportunity for self-definition and rebirth.

Munro, C. Lynn. "The Tattooed Heart and The Serpentine Eye: Morrison's Choice of an Epigraph for *Sula*." *Black American Literature Forum* 18 (Winter 1984): 150–54. Treats Tennessee Williams's play *The Rose Tattoo* as an analog to *Sula*.

Paquet, Sandra Pouchet. "The Ancestor as Foundation in *Their Eyes Were Watching God* and *Tar Baby*." *Callaloo* 13 (1990): 499–515. Discusses Hurston's and Morrison's novels as evidence of the authors' belief in the restorative significance of folk myth and knowledge of ancestry.

Powell, Timothy B. "Toni Morrison: The Struggle to Depict the Black Figure on the White Page." *Black American Literature Forum* 24 (Winter 1990): 747–60. Working with her first three novels, defines Morrison's success in resurrecting the black self, black culture, the black text which have, since slavery, been systematically repressed.

Reddy, Maureen T. "The Tripled Plot and Center of *Sula*." *Black American Literature Forum* 22 (Spring 1988): 29–45. Proposes that *Sula* has not one but three protagonists: Sula/Nel, Shadrack, and the black community. Each of their stories contribute to a central antiwar theme in the novel.

Rosenburg, Ruth. "Seeds in Hard Ground: Black Girlhood in *The Bluest Eye*." *Black American Literature Forum* 21 (Winter 1987): 435–45. General discussion of *The Bluest Eye* as a long-delayed chronicle of black girlhood.

Schmudde, Carol E. "Knowing When to Stop: A Reading of Toni Morrison' *Beloved*." *CLA Journal* 37 (December 1993): 121–35. Discusses the novel's treatment of cultural significance in defining the limits of human suffering.

Smith, Valerie. "The Quest for and Discovery of Identity in Toni Morrison's *Song of Solomon*." *Southern Review* 21 (Summer 1985): 721–32. Examines

Song of Solomon as "the only one of Morrison's [first three] novels in which her protagonist completes successfully his/her search for psychological autonomy" (721).

Stein, Karen F. "Toni Morrison's *Sula:* A Black Woman's Epic." *Black American Literature Forum* 18 (Winter 1984): 146–50. Summary reading of *Sula* as a heroic tale about the black woman's experience.

Story, Ralph. "An Excursion into the Black World: The 'Seven Days' in Toni Morrison's *Song of Solomon*." *Black American Literature Forum* 23 (Spring 1989): 149–58. Focuses on the Seven Days organization in *Song of Solomon* as grounded in contemporary and nineteenth-century black history.

Traylor, Eleanor W. "The Fabulous World of Toni Morrison: Tar Baby." *Confirmation.* Creative and very general reading of *Tar Baby* as a modern fable.

Turner, Darwin T. "Theme, Characterization and Style in the Works of Toni Morrison." In *Black Women Writers (1950–1980): A Critical Evaluation,* Ed. Mari Evans; Intro. Stephen E. Henderson (Garden City, N.Y.: Anchor-Doubleday, 1984): 361–69.

Wong, Shelley. "Transgression as Poesis in *The Bluest Eye*." *Callaloo* 13 (Summer 1990): 471–81. Traces the technical strategies Morrison uses in *The Bluest Eye* to deconstruct European American cultural values that are hostile to blackness and examines the textual strategies used to combat that hostility.

Secondary Bibliography

Middleton, David L. *Toni Morrison: An Annotated Bibliography.* New York: Garland, 1987. Two hundred and twenty-three annotations of anthologies, recordings, reviews, interviews, books, and articles on Morrison. Also lists Morrison's awards, honors, and memberships.

INDEX